MW00685196

BEYOND PRISON

Human Rights in Context

General Editors: **Marguerite Garling**, technical advisor on rights and rule of law and **Guglielmo Verdirame**, University of Cambridge

Research on human rights, or social and political issues closely related to human rights, is nowadays carried out in many academic departments, from law to anthropology, from sociology to philosophy. Yet, there is surprisingly little communication amongst scholars working in these different disciplines, and research that takes more than one perspective into account is seldom encouraged. This new series aims to bridge the divide between the social sciences and the law in human rights scholarship.

Books published in this series will be based on original empirical investigations, innovative theoretical analyses or multidisciplinary research. They will be of interest to all those scholars who seek an audience beyond the confines of their academic subjects.

Volume 1
BETWEEN BOMBS AND GOOD INTENTIONS
The Red Cross and the Italo-Ethiopian War, 1935–1936
Rainer Baudendistel

Volume 2
ADVANCING REFUGEE PROTECTION IN SOUTH AFRICA
Edited by Jeff Handmaker, Lee Anne de la Hunt and Jonathan Klaaren

Volume 3
BEYOND PRISON
The Fight to Reform Prison Systems around the World
Ahmed Othmani

BEYOND PRISON
The Fight to Reform Prison Systems around the World

Ahmed Othmani
with Sophie Bessis

Translated from the French by Marguerite Garling

Berghahn Books
New York • Oxford

Published in 2008 by
Berghahn Books
www.berghahnbooks.com

First published in France as *Sortir de la prison, un combat pour réformer les systèmes carcéraux dans le monde*, Paris.

©Editions LA DÉCOUVERTE, Paris, France, 2002.

Library of Congress Cataloging-in-Publication Data
A C.I.P. catalog record for this book is available from the Library of Congress.

British Library Cataloguing in Publication Data
A catalogue record for this book is available from the British Library

Printed in the United States on acid-free paper.

ISBN: 978-1-84545-454-8 (hardback)

Contents

FOREWORD

Robert Badinter[1]

The world of prisons is one that Ahmed Othmani certainly knew well – not only because he spent nearly ten years of his life in Tunisian jails, but also because of his tireless combat, after leaving prison in 1979, to advance human rights around the world, particularly in the context of prison.

Ahmed Othmani's journey is, in many respects, worthy of admiration. Born in 1943 into a semi-nomadic tribe in Tunisia when it was a French protectorate, he found himself very early on confronted with violence and solitude. The violence was that of the French military who, during the armed struggle of the 1950s, threatened to destroy his parents' home to try and get them to denounce the *fellaghas* fighting for Tunisia's independence.

The solitude he experienced came about because Ahmed Othmani was sent at a very early age to stay with his brother in Tunis to pursue his schooling. From the age of fourteen, he lived on his own in Tunis and all alone there had to succeed in adapting to a totally unknown urban world, surrounded by children of his own age who shared neither his way of life nor his outlook. As a student at Tunis University from 1965, Ahmed Othmani joined the far left group GEAST – Tunisian Socialist Action and Study Group

---

1.   Former French Justice Minister and main instigator of the abolition of the death penalty in France.

– better known by the name of its review, *Perspectives*. There he became an active militant against the one-party dictatorship of Habib Bourguiba. He became acquainted with Michel Foucault, who was then teaching in Tunisia and who, in 1967, hid the young student leader when he was on the run from the police.

After his first arrest in 1968, Ahmed Othmani led a clandestine existence until his second arrest in 1973. Sentenced to twelve years in prison and locked away in solitary confinement, he felt that his life as a free man had come to an end. Once again he had to take on this challenge alone and survive the daily torture sessions to which his jailers subjected him. One of them in particular, whom he calls 'an artist in torture', reserved his very worst treatments for him. But Ahmed Othmani taught himself to resist them, notably by controlling his breathing, so that never once did any of his torturers manage to extract a single word or sound out of him.

During his years in prison, Ahmed Othmani studied as much as he could and subjected himself to a routine of physical exercise so as to maintain his mental and physical capacities. These activities helped him to meet this cruel challenge. The experience transformed him from a youthful opponent of Habib Bourguiba's authoritarian regime into a mature man resolved to pursue his combat by other, 'non-political' forms of militancy.

Freed in 1979, Ahmed Othmani became active in Amnesty International. He had been the first Prisoner of Conscience adopted by the French Section of Amnesty, which had been founded in 1971 during his imprisonment.[2] Ahmed Othmani got very involved in that organisation from 1980 onwards. With his wife Simone, he helped set up the Tunisian Section – the first in the Arab world – and then, in 1984, he took up the new post of development coordinator for Amnesty in the Maghreb and Middle East.

Beyond his work for Prisoners of Conscience, Ahmed Othmani was to remain deeply affected by his prison experience and driven to act in this key area. And so in 1989, with other like-minded people, he founded his own NGO (nongovernmental organisation), Penal Reform International (PRI), with the mandate to 'assist in the adoption of penal reforms, while taking into

2.   By the Tunisian historian Jean-Pierre Darmon and French activist Marie-Josée Protais.

account the diversity of cultural context', in particular through publicity campaigns, support for specific projects and technical advice to local actors. PRI's regional programmes went on to cover every continent.

PRI's competence derives first and foremost from the composition of its staff, a group of seasoned experts drawn from work in prison, as well as its reference to the international legal instruments governing this area of work; and also to the pragmatic spirit which infuses its actions – for PRI never gets involved in any country or region without being sure that there is a real political will to reform and without identifying reliable local contacts, and financial support to ensure that all projects once started can be followed through. PRI's methods have borne fruit, as the success of its projects and their technical expertise attest.

Thus, in the area of legal aid, PRI has supported local bar associations, notably in Pakistan and Malawi, so as to speed up casework and procedures. In some Caribbean countries, PRI has set up a programme of legal aid for Death Row prisoners to allow them to go to appeal or lodge a plea for mercy.

PRI has also invested heavily in a vast programme of prison reform, especially in training prison staff and promoting non-custodial sentencing. An encouraging experience occurred in Zimbabwe as early as the 1980s, with the implementation of community service orders as an alternative to imprisonment. PRI backed the government to help it procure the necessary changes to the Penal Code, identify host institutions to receive those thus sentenced, and set up a network of people to oversee their placements. This model was later exported to other African countries, but also to Latin America and East and Central Europe.

PRI not only works to improve the criminal justice and penal systems; it is active in prevention work too, for example in assisting a local body in Addis Ababa to develop a diversionary project targeting juvenile delinquents.

PRI's programme in Rwanda deserves particular mention. This was started when the country's prisons were bursting with tens of thousands of suspects detained after the 1994 genocide. PRI was, together with the ICRC (International Committee of the Red Cross), the only international organisation carrying out practical work within the prison system. From 1998, PRI played a part in systematically training the entire prison staff, all the way from the warders, through the clerks and accountants to the prison directors, and setting up a system of continuous in-house training. And then PRI's experts addressed themselves to creating productive work inside the prisons, through craft work and prison farms.

The Rwandan government had above all called in PRI to speed up the judicial process and help it to elaborate non-custodial alternative sentencing. A seminar convened by PRI in Rwanda brought together specialists from many countries and this led, in 2000, to the enactment of a law formalising the traditional *gacaca* (grassroots) courts and, more especially, the application of community service sentences.

PRI's work, without doubt, serves as an indispensable complement to that of intergovernmental organisations such as the European Committee for the Prevention of Torture and Inhuman or Degrading Treatment or Punishment (CPT), set up under the 1987 Convention of the same name. The CPT's independent experts visit places of detention every year to assess the treatment of those detained in the forty-three states that are parties to this Convention. They are permitted to speak in confidence with the detainees and can, if need be, formulate specific recommendations in their reports.

Likewise, the vote at the 58th Session of the Committee for Human Rights in Geneva[3] (18 March to 26 April 2002) is to be welcomed: it resolved to adopt a draft Optional Protocol to the 1984 UN Convention against Torture and Other Cruel, Inhuman or Degrading Treatment or Punishment, which would set up a preventive mechanism of regular visits to places of detention in all countries ratifying the Protocol.[4]

This significant progress is to be applauded, as is the appearance of this modest book, which is the remarkable culmination of a life of reflection and committed action undertaken over more than forty years by a man of honour and conviction.

Editor's note: Ahmed Othmani was killed in a hit and run road accident in Morocco on 8 December 2004.

---

3.   Superseded by the Council on Human Rights in 2006.
4.   Adopted in 2002.

PREFACE
Mary Robinson

I was very pleased as UN High Commissioner for Human Rights to contribute to the publication of Ahmed Othmani's book, 'Sortir de la prison, un combat pour réformer les systèmes carcéraux dans le monde'. (*Beyond Prison: The Fight to Reform Prison Systems around the World*). Ahmed came to see me a number of times in Geneva, and I was deeply impressed by his passion and commitment to penal reform. Later, when in my current work as President of Realizing Rights I invited Ahmed to attend a seminar on human rights in South Africa, he turned the tables and persuaded me to serve as Honorary President of Penal Reform International! It was an honour to value publicly the work of Ahmed and his colleagues.

This is an exceptional personal testimony and story of achievement. Ahmed Othmani tells of his own appalling treatment when in detention and how it informed and inspired a lifetime vocation to struggle for the rights of all prisoners, everywhere. As the story demonstrates, Othmani was one of those rare individuals who moved from passion and conviction to effective action - he was responsible for the establishment of one of the world's most reliable and mature human rights organisations, in the field of penal reform, Penal Reform International (PRI). His untimely death in Morocco in 2004 deprived the cause of a passionate advocate, but the work goes on.

I share the great concern which Ahmed Othmani had and PRI continues to have for the world's prisoners. Often voiceless and forgotten, prisoners are among the most vulnerable groups in any society. Time and time again they are subjected to multiple abuses of their human rights and are provided with little or no means to seek redress.

The United Nations continues to take steps to highlight the plight of prisoners, to articulate minimum standards for detention, to decry arbitrary detention and to support national efforts to improve prison conditions. This work would have only limited impact were it not carried out in partnership with international civil society. I welcome, therefore, the increasing collaboration which the United Nations – and especially the Office of High Commissioner for Human Rights – has developed with PRI. I trust that they will continue to be constructive partners in the years to come.

I hope people everywhere, including prisoners, will have the opportunity to read this book. It deserves attention, as it makes an important case for accountability as well as rehabilitation, and the long-term protection of societies and individuals. This is a message which should be heard in prisons and at the level of policy-making nationally and internationally.

New York, November 2006

1

JOURNEY OF A GENERATION

Ahmed Othmani was born in 1943 in Tunisia, at the edge of the open plains and the desert. Tunisia, a small country at once profoundly Arabic yet open to the Mediterranean, was a French protectorate from 1881 to 1956, noted for its urban elites, which rapidly embraced modern living, and for Habib Bourguiba, its outstanding figurehead. Ahmed started his schooling at the beginning of independence, at a time when a whole generation was gaining access to education for the first time. Through his education, this child of nomadic parents brought up in a world ruled by tradition, became over time a left-wing intellectual and an activist.

Although apparently atypical, his journey was nevertheless representative of the 1960s, a time when young people worldwide burst onto the political scene. In countries all over the Third World, the preceding generation had spent their youth fighting colonial domination; but by May 1968, young people the world over would experience disillusionment, either deserting the political arena or being side-tracked into the quest for identity or religious belief. Steering a course between the two, the internationalist militants of the 1960s and 1970s were determined to bring about a revolution on their own home soil.

In Tunisia, the Groupe d'études et d'action socialiste tunisien (GEAST) – better known as Perspectives after the name of their magazine – embodied the Tunisian far left of this time. After 1968, the terrible repression which hit the movement saw its leaders and many militants imprisoned, some for more than ten years, among

*them Ahmed Othmani. From this bitter experience, they kept a
strong sense of commitment, many of them inspired by it to
become human rights activists in the ensuing decades. In the
South, where countries had since independence only experienced
authoritarian regimes, this proved to be another equally viable
form of political activism.*

*The route followed by Ahmed Othmani epitomises the hopes,
suffering and disillusionment of his contemporaries. It is the story
of a militant, reflecting the ambiguities of Bourguiba's reign, and
the story of a generation of young people ready to face any risk
and to sacrifice everything to change the old world order. It also
allows us to understand how the experience of prison can shape
the life of a human being.*

From the arid plains to the city

I come from southern Tunisia, from the arid lands good only for
rearing livestock; colonial agriculture took up the most fertile
lands. From the early twentieth century, tribes – including my own
– were dispossessed and driven back to the poorest land, which is
the arid plains. During my childhood, the years of armed struggle
for independence left their mark on me, the most active resistance
being in my region, between Gafsa and Sidi Bou Zid. This was the
land of the fighters known as *fellaghas*, who included several
members of my extended family. Armed groups often stopped at
our place, and I often went with older relatives to take food to
them in the mountains. I saw at close range the tanks and aircraft
used by the French during the 1950s. When I was ten years old,
some soldiers threatened to burn down my parents' tent to force
them to denounce the *fellaghas*.

It is from this nomadic world that my family hails. My family
has historically established Hilali origins.[1] My father, although the
youngest of several brothers, was the real head of the family. He
learned to read and write at the age of thirty, at the same time as

---

1.   In the mid-eleventh century, the Arab Beni Hilal tribes arrived in North
     Africa, driven from Egypt by the Fatimid caliphate. It was these Hilali
     invasions and not the conquest itself that changed the demographic
     make-up of the Maghreb, enhancing its Arab component. People of Hilali
     origin are seen as Arabs, in contrast to the Berber tribes.

his children. My family was steeped in oral tradition. We learned by rote the works of poets from Arabia and Yemen or the Hilali saga, which was a history of expeditions and raids. We lived on horseback. This type of society has always cultivated a fierce independence, recognising no other authority than the clan's. Central government had hardly any influence on our lives. The clan was self-governing, and patriarchal authority ruled over the extended family. Up until the 1960s, we had no idea what police or prisons were. As for the academic background of our leaders, it came obviously from Zitouna.[2] From my earliest years, I was surrounded by men who had studied at Zitouna and who were always talking politics.

When I think of my early adolescence, I remember it as a strange journey: at thirteen I left the freedom of the open range, the trails and mountains, the horse or camel treks following the herds and the tent that we pitched each day in a different place. I was suddenly plucked from an increasingly sedentary tribal life and transported to the solitude of the big city. The children of my own age that I met there had nothing in common with me, except for sharing the same school benches and listening to the same teachers.

From the age of fourteen, after spending a few months with my elder brother, I lived completely alone in Tunis, and I learned to take care of myself. I coped all on my own with the break from the tribal world which I had come from. While I learned the rules of urban living, I felt different and solitary. I was a puny, impecunious child, who did not play the same games as other children of my age around me. La Goulette, where I lived, was nevertheless a rather special and more open place in those days. Sicilian fishermen inhabited the Little Sicily quarter with its church, near where I lived when I first arrived. Assumption Day, 15 August, when the statue of the Virgin Mary was paraded around, was a holiday for all the inhabitants of La Goulette – the other Italians, the Greeks and Maltese too. As for the Jews, they were the majority in those days, while the grocers were all from Djerba.

2. Most of the Arabic-speaking elites of Tunisia and Algeria were educated at the theological university of Zitouna until it was closed down by Bourguiba at independence.

My arrival in the capital coincided with the euphoria of independence, and I had the feeling of being actively involved in my country's liberation. But 1955 and 1956 were marked by a major schism that shook Tunisia – the split between Habib Bourguiba and Salah Ben Youssef, number two in the Néo-Destour party.[3] Ben Youssef symbolised for us the Arab Orient, Nasser, and the first nonaligned conference in Bandung, where he represented his party. Bourguiba, on the other hand, was deeply influenced by French modernity and never embraced Arab nationalism. To a certain extent, Ben Youssef's dissidence set the citydwellers against the semi-nomadic world of the Tunisian South, the *makhzen* against the *siba*, as the Moroccans would say.

When I arrived in Tunis in 1956, historical events and France had decided in favour of Bourguiba. We all knew that he meant modernity: in other words, something totally new for someone like me coming from a tribal background. My father repudiated his first wife and later took two wives. Polygamy was still practised in my part of the world, even though it was rare. Yet one of the first decisions Bourguiba took was to abolish it. This modern way of doing things soon won me over. It wasn't him I fought against later, but the one-party system.

However, my brother, the one who decided my fate by bringing me to the capital, had a strong Arab-Muslim streak which he shared with some of the old urban elites. In fact, he nearly disappeared during the dark days when Bourguiba's militia was redoubling its illegal killings of suspected Youssefists. Thus the euphoria of the years 1955–56 was also a time of great tension, heightened by the spreading war in neighbouring Algeria. It was in the summer of 1956 that the main FLN (Front de Libération Nationale) leaders were kidnapped, when the airplane taking them from Rabat to Tunis was forced to land by the French. Finally, 1956 was the year in which the Suez Canal was nationalised and war ensued. That, too, was a major event.

In my early adolescence I began to absorb French and Western culture, having mastered the French language that I had barely

3.   The Tunisian Constitutionalist Party, or Destour in Arabic, was set up in 1920 using the first nationalist slogans. Habib Bourguiba became a member at the end of the 1920s, but left in 1934 to found the Néo-Destour Party, which took Tunisia to independence under his leadership.

known on my arrival in Tunis. I read everything that came my way. As I lived alone, a few of my teachers took me under their wing, suggesting what to read and inviting me to their homes. Many had progressive ideas. They introduced me to Malraux, Hemingway, Sartre, Camus and Simone de Beauvoir. They influenced me a lot and I soon identified with their way of thinking.

Later, with friends from different schools in Tunis, girls as well as boys, we set up a philosophical discussion group, which was my first venture into intellectual life. At the time, we did not touch directly on political issues, but we were driven by a strong determination to reject the control of the already all-powerful Destour youth organisation. Moreover, nearly all the members of this group have retained their critical distance from the ruling party ever since and have never subscribed to the one-party state.

Starting in politics

In 1965, the university was the scene of heated public debate. Political power, democracy, social inequality and imperialism were all discussed at length. In showing our support for the Vietnamese in their struggle against the United States, we came out against Bourguiba, who had sided firmly with the Americans. For the student protest movement, of which I was spokesman, Vietnam symbolised the anti-imperialist struggle, along with Cuba. We followed the emergence of the Black Panther movement closely, as well as the UCLA sit-ins against the Vietnam war. We young left-wing Tunisians were fascinated by everything that happened in the outside world: in today's terms, we were 'globalised'. It was at that time that I joined the GEAST, which most closely matched my aspirations.

One of the most important events of that period was the Arab-Israeli war of June 1967, which marked a high point in the history of the Tunisian left. On the first day of that war, in the afternoon of 15 June, we were actually confronted with the beginnings of a pogrom in Tunis. We left-wing militants marching in support of Palestine were the only ones who tried to stop the demonstration descending into anti-Jewish violence, which the police did nothing to prevent. Yet my generation had since 1956 been literally lulled into believing the war of words raging over the airwaves between Bourguiba and Nasser's triumphant Arab nationalism. At the time,

Nasser's stand was praised as a heroic deed of the anti-imperialist struggle, and we condemned Bourguiba's stance alongside the Americans. But neither were we won over by Nasser's Arabist rhetoric. Our twin adherence to Marxism and to Bourguiba's modernism played a large part in this. Nasser, on the other hand, was close to the Soviet Union, which we were already beginning to criticise.

We felt closer to the Chinese than to the Soviets, having read Althusser. To accept the Chinese theories meant to us a return to the purity of Marxist thought. So we naturally fell in with the international student non-conformists, who saw themselves as countering orthodox Stalinism and the misappropriation of Marx and early Lenin by the USSR. We discoursed at length about the role of the proletariat in countries of the Third World. In fact, we felt closest to the revolutionary movements which occurred in the South, from China to Cuba. We admired Mehdi Ben Barka (the Moroccan opposition politician), and we read *Révolution africaine*, the Algerian magazine edited until 1965 by Mohammed Harbi. We followed Che Guevara, and all those others who inspired new hopes for our country.

As internationalists we did not turn to Arab nationalist thinkers for guidance. The defeat of Nasser in 1967 confirmed us in our beliefs. We remained unmoved when the Arab street urged him to remain in power; but, even before then, the gap between us and our fellow students steeped in Arab nationalism had been widening. For it was in 1967 that we had published our famous 'Yellow Book' on the Palestinian question.

Writing this pamphlet marked an important phase in our thinking. We did in fact find ourselves in tune with Bourguiba's position on Palestine in 1965, when he claimed that two states should co-exist within the former Palestine mandate. We pushed our international approach to its logical limit by recognising that two nationalities existed in that territory and therefore advocating its partition. We weren't worried about being called pro-Zionist: in 1966, *Perspectives* had been the first to publish the 1965 Fatah positions in Tunisia. However, we always kept our distance from the nationalists who saw the Palestinian combat as a purely Arab cause, since we saw it as a national liberation struggle. With hindsight, I think that the reason we dared to go further than the others was because our movement was so young. We had no past to come to terms with, and we were not accountable to the mainstream right or left. Our group included people from different backgrounds, with a range of personal histories and experience, who came together around a common politically and ideologically non-conformist stance.

We had no qualms either about opposing Ahmed Ben Salah's autocratic land reforms that imposed forced collectivisation, which the Tunisian communists rallied to. Instead, we put out a public critique of it.

Another pamphlet dealt with the nature of the state. Obviously our line about the dictatorship of the proletariat smacks of totalitarianism nowadays, but we did raise real issues, even though they were couched in the language of the day. In fact, we initiated the beginnings of a Tunisian approach to all the key questions in those days. Where we were a bit schizophrenic was in denouncing the Tunisian one-party state while advocating the dictatorship of the proletariat as the way to world revolution.

Actually, there were several tendencies within the GEAST on that issue. Many of us were influenced by Maoism. Others were more pragmatic and focused their thoughts on the nature of democracy. We opposed the Destour party on issues of freedom of expression, the one-party state, and democracy. But we also subscribed to the Lenin who wrote *What Is To Be Done?*

Our political discussions were lively, but we didn't discuss social questions very much. This was because Tunisia was a country deeply affected by Bourguiba's modern ideas. You may recall his weekly radio broadcasts in which he addressed Tunisians like a schoolmaster, using the vernacular to make his modern ideas accessible to all. This was the Bourguiba who urged people not to fast so as to save their strength for the development effort, and who would publicly quench his thirst at mid-day during Ramadan. It was he who made Tunisia the only Arab country to have abolished polygamy and repudiation, and who accorded women a number of rights.

Our group was socially, ethnically and religiously mixed. Even if many of us were from modest backgrounds, most were city-based intellectuals. In fact, we had nothing to say about social issues. Bourguiba had pre-empted us, but in a positive way: we were in agreement with him. We concurred even more with his educational policies, which revolutionised Tunisia. We thus felt at ease in a country where, in societal matters, progressive ideas prevailed.

Cultural discussions and intellectual debates, on the other hand, were part of our daily life. With Jean-Pierre Darmon, a professor of ancient history and later a founding member of Amnesty International's French Section, we discussed Athenian democracy. Jean Gattegno, trade unionist and English specialist, with whom I stayed for several months, shared his views on union issues, literature and music. Michel Foucault's stay in Tunisia from 1966 to 1968 left its mark on us as well. He not only taught at the university in Tunis, but also gave public lectures once a week in the main lecture theatre, where you had to arrive early to get a seat. He was close to us: in 1967, during demonstrations against the visit of U.S. Vice-President Hubert Humphrey, I hid at his place as I was one of the student leaders police were looking for. He was later a witness at our trial in September 1968; or, more precisely, he lodged a request to testify in my favour, which the judges rejected. We used to run off our political tracts at his house in Sidi Bou Saïd. Following our trial, he decided not to renew his contract, and left Tunisia. It is this experience which may in part explain Foucault's enduring interest in detention and prison conditions.

From activism to repression

Our generation, Communists and Ba'athists[4] included, left its own mark on Tunisia. The years 1966–68 marked the high point of the worldwide student movement against imperialism, with a strong strain of ideological radicalism critical of Soviet 'revisionism' – even leading intellectuals like Sartre were caught up in it. This radicalisation was widely reflected in the Tunisian student movement and the most radical group within *Perspectives* was thus able to impose its views. However, when the clampdown began, we all found ourselves together behind bars, whatever differences of opinion we may have had.

This generation was in fact far ahead of its home public in believing that it could bridge the gap between the old world order and the new. Moreover, at the end of the 1960s, Tunisian society

4.   The Ba'ath Party, founded in 1943 by Michal Aflak, the Syrian proponent of Arab nationalism, had a strong influence on Tunisian students, some of whom for a long time claimed allegiance to his ideas.

was faced with enormous problems arising from the policy of forced collectivisation. On these issues, our tiny group found a huge audience through its writings and activism. The regime felt seriously threatened because our vision – however far-fetched or ridiculous it may appear nowadays – was diametrically opposed to that of the government. Many saw the extremity of our opposition as the only way to stop the government's programme drifting out of control. We represented something totally different that questioned the very foundations of the regime.

I remember evening meetings in Jendouba in 1966 with dozens of cooperative farmers who told me how they could have created workable cooperatives themselves instead of being forced into an unwanted collectivisation. Paradoxically, in taking fright, the authorities helped us: by overestimating our importance they made us better known. They attributed to us a sphere of influence far greater than was really the case. Thus, a handful of left-wing activists grouped within *Perspectives* enjoyed a much greater impact than anyone could have dreamed of.

In a headlong reaction, the government threw itself into the construction of its so-called socialism by accelerating the process of collectivisation. The one-party system had lost much of its legitimacy after the extremely brutal repression of the 1962 coup attempt.[5] Bourguiba tarnished his reputation by executing men who had come to symbolise the independence struggle, but who had made the mistake of being Youssefists or of simply opposing him. The collectivist error had lost the government the backing it enjoyed from the rural and commercial lower middle classes. In 1968, it was the upper middle class, led by former Justice and Defence Minister Ahmed Mestiri, which went into opposition.

In this context, the student movement could be seen as a threat, all the more so as our group was becoming more and more visibly active. One of *Perspectives'* leaders, Mohammed Ben Jennet, had been arrested and sentenced to forced labour following the events of June 1967. Being a graduate of Zitouna, perfectly fluent in

---

5.   The bloody battle of Bizerta (July 1961) was followed by the assassinaton in Frankfurt of Salah Youssef (for a long time number two of the Neo-Destour) who, from his Cairo exile, had ceaselessly exhorted Tunisians to revolt against Bourguiba. This increased the hostility of part of the army to Bourguiba's government. A military plot was revealed in December 1962 and most of the plotters executed in January 1963.

Arabic, and a good public speaker capable of rousing the massed students, he was seen by the government as someone to be brought down; but as a symbol, he had become a mobilising force, increasing the following of *Perspectives* within the student movement.

In 1966, several leaders of the student left were arbitrarily called up for military service. Since 1967, the student movement – mobilised around issues of democracy, freedom of expression and association, and against the stifling of civil society by the one-party state – had continued to grow in power until the protests of March 1968 began. All universities were at a standstill with the strikes, and the movement was beginning to affect secondary and primary schools. The agitation was reaching the streets. *Perspectives* was carrying out fly-posting campaigns in the working-class areas. We had very simple printing methods which allowed us to distribute our tracts and flood whole sections of the city with our materials; by morning, the buses were covered in our posters. The fact that our tracts were in vernacular Arabic made us even more of a threat in the government's eyes. The effervescence was at its height: left-wing activists occupied the new university and the institutes of higher education. That was when the authorities decided to hit back.

I was first arrested on 18 March with a colleague by members of the party militia called out to suppress the student movement. The workers were also mobilised, as the UGTT[6] under Habib Achour was at that time under the complete control of the ruling party. In 1972, Achour called my future wife Simone Lellouche 'Tunisia's answer to Daniel Cohn-Bendit' (leader of the student protesters in France). On the evening of the 18th, we were taken to the Tunis headquarters of the Néo-Destour coordinating committee, in the Kasbah. After receiving a thorough beating, we were thrown into the street unconscious, in the middle of the night. That was the militia's usual way of doing things in those days.

But our real arrest occurred the next day, during a meeting in the Dean's office. Actually, I was one of the student leaders who

---

6.   Union Générale des Travailleurs de Tunisie, Tunisia's single labour union, which had, since independence, alternated between autonomy from and subordination to the Néo-Destour.

was negotiating with the university authorities for the release of Ben Jennet and other comrades arrested after him, and for guarantees of the students' right to form unions. The Tunisian 'May '68' thus came to an end two months before it started in France.

Then began a new round of interrogations, torture and massive repression, with dozens of arrests. The most difficult period for me lasted two and a half months. I first passed through the hands of the *Direction de la Sécurité du Territoire* (DST), then I was transferred to E block of the 9th April Prison[7] together with political prisoners and those sentenced to death. I was taken out of my cell to the DST or to former colonial farms on the outskirts of Tunis which had been converted into torture centres. That's where they tortured us in water-filled cellars. This inhuman treatment lasted until our trial in September 1968.

The experience of torture

That was my first real encounter with systematic violence. However, the most difficult time I had was not during my 1968 arrest, but in 1973. At the time, I was holed up in a hiding-place that was given away under torture by one of our comrades. In the middle of the night, while I slept, some sixty armed police led by the director of the DST raided the house. At the Ministry of the Interior I ran the gauntlet of a series of police officers who spat at me, hit me and pulled at my moustache. They vented their anger on me after searching for me for so long. They drank wine and danced around while I was being tortured at the hands of a real torture virtuoso, notorious among former prisoners for using pliers to tear off skin, and who reserved his most sophisticated techniques for us. These tortures in 1973 went on for longer than in 1968, but were intermittent. As I was weakened by successive hunger strikes, they left me some moments of respite to recover. They would leave me alone in a cell, chained by my hands and feet. Then they would start again. Among other things, they burned my skin with ether and let the wounds get infected.

7.   The Civil Prison situated on the Boulevard du 9 avril in Tunis. It was demolished in March 2007.

That was when I acquired the ability to resist pain by learning to cut myself off from any kind of physical sensation. I no longer felt anything, even at the sight of my own blood. I had to prepare for such states of mind. At the height of violence and pain, I had to learn to tell myself it didn't matter. It also became a sort of challenge addressed to my torturers as well as to myself. I never spoke to them, I never screamed; and this drove them mad, to the point where one of them beat me five hundred times on the soles of my feet to try and get a sound out of me. They would have preferred any expression of feeling, including hatred, than nothing at all; but I closed myself off entirely from them and from the feeling of pain.

When they realised that I resisted by controlling my breathing, they responded with drops from a bottle onto my nostrils, preventing any control over my breathing. It was a struggle between two forces: one puny man with no strength left resisting a machine unable to crush him. The strangest thing, though, was that my torturers would sometimes chat to each other when they thought I was unconscious. They would talk about their children, their families, their career prospects. They would call up their girlfriends. In other words, they behaved like just ordinary human beings, even though they committed the worst atrocities without any hesitation or pang of conscience.

To hold out, I had to resist at two levels: physically resist of course; but also fight against the degradation and denial of humanity that are inherent in the act of torture. The sense of my own human dignity, at once physical and moral, gave me the strength to resist and put aside pain and suffering at the hardest points. At no time did I draw strength from religion. Many of those subjected to the same treatment took refuge in religion during the most difficult moments, sometimes resorting to primitive forms of religious behaviour, in a kind of blind faith which freed them from their doubts and anguish. As for me, my self-respect and sense of dignity saved me, by allowing me never to speak in front of my torturers. In a way, the experience of torture transformed my abstract belief in the importance of human dignity into a concrete first-hand experience of it. Having said that, I would never condemn those who cracked up or wrote letters begging for pardon, in order to be released. Sometimes the degree of suffering or the pressures on their family were too much, and nobody is infallible.

Out of this experience, I have retained an awareness of the complexity of human nature. I was kept under police guard around the clock. One day, before leaving, one of them embraced me with tears running down his face, having just seen his colleague urinate on me in a fit of rage because he couldn't get me to speak. Some behaved like the SS while others, torn with remorse, were disgusted by the treatment inflicted on me. Some managed never to lay a finger on me, even though they did the same job and received the same orders as my torturers.

What's more, I kept in touch with some of them later on. Whenever they could, they showed their sympathy for me. It was mainly the ordinary policemen on guard at the DST who were most troubled by my treatment. As I was held there for several months, we ended up recognising each other. During my 1971–72 detention, I even managed to have discussions with some of them. I tried to explain to them that it was my right to express my opinion, that I had never advocated violence, nor had I ever held any weapons, and that by rights I shouldn't be in prison. They replied that they didn't know the law – all they knew was Bourguiba.

It was at that time that I began to recognise that political pluralism was a necessary counterweight to the unchecked power of the state. For, like my colleagues, I had long been rather schizophrenic in claiming all rights and freedoms for myself while advocating the dictatorship of the proletariat.

The experience of prison

The first challenge in prison is solitude. At the start of my second stay in Borj Erroumi, the prison fortress in Bizerta, I was kept in total isolation, completely cut off from the outside world. One day, one of the common-law prisoners trusted by the authorities was standing guard on the roof of the small building where I was held, and addressed a couple of words to me. He was immediately clapped in chains in a dungeon, with his head shaved, because nobody had the right to speak to me. In spite of this, there were always times when I managed to communicate with the outside world,[8] especially as I already knew the prison from our previous detention in 1969–70.

The other main challenge was over-crowding. It may seem strange that this should have bothered me, after being kept in total isolation, but that is how it was. In prison you experience extremes. From 1974, I was put back in the communal cell. The crowding was unbearable. We were all crammed in on top of each other. At one point there were thirty of us in one small room. Most of us smoked, although the room had only two skylights. The air was thick with smoke. Ever since my stay at the DST in 1971, I suffered constant breathing problems and allergies. And ever since my time in that shared cell, I could never stand tobacco smoke.

Moreover, there was a total lack of privacy and it was impossible to keep clean. We quarrelled all the time over trifles, not to mention our political differences, which grew more and more acute in that closed-off world. Baathists, communists, first- and second-generation members of *Perspectives*, all shared that one cell. I could hardly bear my own company. Two things helped me to hold out: I worked a lot at night while the others slept, on a correspondence course in economics at the University of Paris-VIII, and I did four hours of exercise every day.

The government never formally recognised us as political prisoners, which prompted repeated and interminable hunger-strikes on our part. As soon as one started, the authorities would lock us away in cells, barefoot even in the middle of winter, and having to sleep on the bare cement floor without any blanket or covering. We were force-fed as soon as we began to weaken. Bit by bit, however, we won some rights. From 1976, we could watch television and in 1978 we were allowed to cook our own meals.

Throughout our time in prison, we were in contact with common-law prisoners. For a few days in 1971, I even shared a cell with a man condemned to death and I saw him taken away for execution. He was a peasant farmer from the North-West, accused of killing his wife and two children, though he claimed he was innocent and even got me to write a letter to the President's wife about it. I do not know to this day if he was really innocent, but I

8.   On one occasion, Ahmed Othmani sent a detailed critique of Amnesty International's Annual Report to the organisation from inside Borj Erroumi [Editor's note].

am sure he would never have killed anyone in cold blood. I could see the weight of his contradictions, his immense moral suffering and his extreme poverty. This prompted some intense soul-searching on my part, as I spent whole nights talking to him, and sounding out his deepest inner self.

We were also in close contact with ordinary prisoners doing the cleaning and bringing us food sent in by our families. They would run errands for us, paid for with cigarettes and items of clothing. We knew about their wretched cells, which up to 150 of them shared at any one time, and which were always run by a cell boss and his mafia.

The guards also told us about prison life, and we ended up knowing all about it: the trafficking, the tortures, the beatings and mistreatment. The two main commodities traded in prison are sex and cigarettes. The worst thing is the power held by the cell bosses at the behest of the prison authorities. Unlike the guards, they never leave their victims alone and have sole power to decide who will be bullied, who will sleep next to the latrines, or whose turn it is to be raped that evening. No youngster in prison can avoid this. When the boss decides on it, everything is arranged, as in a brothel: a blanket is hung across a corner of the room and a cashier receives payment in money or cigarettes from the clients.

The prison guards and the authorities are well aware of this underground life in prison. Everybody takes part in the illicit trading. And it is the same everywhere. In all the prisons in all the countries I visit nowadays, I find the same things going on that I have seen or known myself. This knowledge has made me extremely sensitive to prison conditions in general, not only those of political prisoners. From long experience I retain an acute sense of the price of freedom and justice.

I have also come to the conclusion that the rule of law must always be upheld. Those who fall victim to unlawful arrest must be able to refer to it, but those who are entrusted with applying it should also know and respect it. They have to understand that the law isn't only there to repress or punish, but also to ensure that the rights of those who are at fault should be respected. Certainly there has to be order in prisons, but prisoners also have a right to protection.

If prisons are officially considered as the place where those who have upset the social order should mend their ways, then the right conditions for this must be created. Yet imprisonment contains a

major contradiction within itself. On the one hand, it creates
dependence: you eat, sleep, piss and wash at set times, in a life
devoid of any responsibility. This removal of responsibility, this
infantilisation, runs counter to any idea of rehabilitation or social
reintegration: in prison, you don't decide anything save what is
forbidden; the only surviving freedom resides in transgression.

This way of thinking only occurred to me later on. It also drew
on my reading. In prison, I read all the recently published accounts
of the Soviet Gulag, as well as those of the Soledad Brothers in
America.[9] During my last years in prison, I thus stored up my own
observations, the results of my reading and some intense moments
of reflection on the meaning of individual responsibility and the
arbitrary nature of absolute power.

Then, on the other hand, time wears you down in prison. The
passage of time was marked by the sun's movement and the
moment when it reached our skylight. It was through light
entering our cell that we could measure time. And then, it is time's
duration which prisoners always have mixed feelings about,
depending on their mood. Both times I was sentenced – in 1968
and 1973 – I started by writing to my wife Simone asking her to
forget about me and get on with her life. These letters were
actually intercepted by the prison authorities and so she only read
them after my release. And, some thirty-four years later, here we
are still together... At the time, I was convinced that my life as a
free man was at an end. But hope never dies. These alternating
moods of hope and resignation are an inescapable part of life in
prison.

You can also project yourself onto others. During my years in
detention, I kept up a continuous correspondence with my young
nephews and nieces. Time in prison was also punctuated by the
small pleasures of life, such as taking a shower, the arrival of food-
parcels or money-orders, or a visit from the doctor. It is only on
leaving prison that you realise how time has stood still inside it.

9.   The notorious trial of the three 'Soledad Brothers', sentenced to heavy
      prison terms in the United States, marked the struggle of black Americans
      in the 1960s. George Jackson got life imprisonment in 1961 for stealing
      70 dollars and was assassinated in prison in 1971, a year after one of his
      brothers. His book, *Soledad Brothers*, was published in French with a
      preface by Jean Genet.

In your mind, you know that things outside the prison are changing. But inside, social relations with other people, with family and friends, are frozen. They change, but we don't. Prisoners expect, in some atavistic, subconscious way, that their family and friends will stay the same, that they will behave and react in the same way as before. But that is impossible. It is then that disaster may strike. Personal tragedies enveloped some of our friends on their release from prison, ending in divorce or even, in a few cases, in suicide.

A different way of learning about politics

Paradoxically, prison also means the discovery of others through the solidarity they express. There were two stages of solidarity for us. At first, it wasn't shown to us as individuals. We were just a group of university students and teachers up against an authoritarian regime based on the one-party system. All we demanded was freedom, democracy, and the right to freedom of expression and to have our own free union. We had not been arrested as individuals, but as members of a larger movement with international dimensions. When we were tortured in April 1968, we knew that Alain Geismar, then Secretary General of the French university teachers' union SNES-Sup, had come to Tunis to support us. We knew that people like the agronomist René Dumont and world-famous academics who had taught some of us were mobilising in our favour. International support for us was soon organised, especially in France where committees were set up to defend us.

This initial solidarity was much more political than at the human rights level. It was during our trial in September 1968 that I first heard about Amnesty International, which had sent an observer. Then, when Amnesty's French Section was set up in 1971, I was adopted as their first prisoner of conscience. Amnesty International's support opened up new horizons for us. We received their reports and dozens of letters written by Amnesty members, which were sent to me clandestinely. I spent hours answering them one by one. And that's actually how I came to write my torture testimony. I got into correspondence with a Swedish lady who wrote as a member of an Amnesty group. We had started to write to each other regularly and one day I just

wrote down my account of the tortures all in one go. I sent it to
Simone on a flimsy piece of paper to forward it, and, with the help
of a few friends, she managed to get it published.[10]

That was how, while in prison, I discovered another form of
activism that was not directly political. In Tunisia, this type of
activism began in 1977, when the Tunisian Human Rights League
was set up. While in prison, we had been kept informed about
preparations for this and six of us sent a clandestine letter of
support for this initiative, which was read out during the inaugural
meeting of the League. This 'non-political' activism took a long
time to take root. For a long time, even Amnesty International
only involved itself with political prisoners. Its campaigns against
the death penalty and against torture in general, which
encompassed greater numbers of people, only came to prominence
later.[11]

10. Ahmed Ben Othman, 'Répression en Tunisie' in *Les Temps Modernes*,
     April 1979.
11. Amnesty's international campaign against torture started in 1973, its
     death penalty campaign *c.* 1977 [Editor's note].

2

FROM REVOLUTION TO THE DEFENCE OF FREEDOM

The former members of Perspectives *were released from prison on 3 August 1979 after almost a decade in detention, during which time Tunisia underwent important changes. It changed course after Ahmed Ben Salah's socialist experiment failed and Hedi Nouira liberalised the economy. It experienced an unquestionable growth in wealth, which brought into being a real middle class. A more educated working class with more working women also emerged, with the spectacular development of manufacturing industry.*

Alongside these transformations, the political scene was reconstituted. The revolutionary far left was marginalised, as everywhere else in the world, while two new players emerged: a civil society actively pursuing the democratisation of politics, and an Islamist movement whose supporters were on the increase. The late 1970s thus saw several generations meeting up within the Tunisian Human Rights League, created in May 1977. These were biological generations, of course, but also successive generations of militants, coming from different political horizons. In it were defectors from the single party, disaffected over the issue of basic freedoms, and former communists and left-wing radicals. All these people came together around a few strong ideas: democracy, human rights, freedom of expression and political pluralism. In fact, the transition of the first generation of Perspectives *intellectuals from revolutionary activism to the defence of democratic ideals and the human rights that go with them, was part of a wider movement that went beyond the Tunisian context. But, if the decline of revolutionary ideology was a worldwide phenomenon, in the Arab world it was accompanied by the growing power of political Islam.*

It is in this context, very different from that of the late 1960s, that Ahmed Othmani reappeared as a free man and an activist. Henceforth, with no illusions but ever ready to defend the principles for which he had given over ten years of his life, it was beyond Tunisia and in the wider world that he tried to make them a reality. After devoting much of the 1980s to working for Amnesty International, in 1989, he and a few like-minded colleagues set up Penal Reform International (PRI).

Quite apart from the personal history which had prepared him for this new commitment, the coming into being of this organisation also shows how political and social thinking about the world of prisons had changed. Not only were political prisoners no longer the only ones to be considered, but – starting from the 1980s – the focus of analysis gradually shifted from the fate of the prisoner to the prison system itself. The universal character of human rights means that no category of human being should be denied them, even those whose acts exclude them from society. Everywhere, people were becoming aware that prison is not a world situated beyond the bounds of society and that its inmates also have rights. The creation of PRI was inspired to a great extent by this belief. This new body was thus clearly situated within the defence of human rights. But, unlike its predecessors, it worked as a development NGO, with well-defined projects and programmes, all of which aim to introduce rights and the rule of law into the jungle of prison life.

This vast programme of action transcends all divisions, including the North-South divide. For, contrary to what a good section of public opinion in the North thinks, barbaric practices in prison are far from being the sole prerogative of the South, even if it is true that there are more despotic governments there. By opening up new directions in the defence of human rights, PRI thus also set itself new challenges.

In praise of pluralism

We must hark back to the years in prison to understand how and why so many *Perspectives* militants changed course politically. During the 1970s, at the same time that our country was undergoing this transformation, the GEAST set off down a path of radicalisation which led to a populist impasse and impoverished its thinking. In the 1960s, it was more a movement of intellectuals, coming up with theories and attempting to analyse society but without any real constituency among the people. By contrast, during the 1970s it became a movement of protest with more popular backing.

At the university, the new context gave rise to violence, with the emergence of a group of students who foreshadowed the Islamic movement; indeed, some of them later became leaders of the *Mouvement de la tendance islamique* (Islamic Tendency Movement). These developments led to deepening rifts among the activist groups. In the end, what was left of the movement fell into the hands of the populists, helped along by official repression as its intellectual core group was in prison. And it was in prison that we took up our position against this divergent trend, which led in turn to the break-up of *Perspectives* and the birth of the left-wing populist movement *Amel Tounsi*.[1]

The reason for all this was because our democratic and pluralist beliefs had been reinforced throughout our last three years in prison. After the first cracks appeared in 1974–75, the rift widened to such an extent that a break-up was on the cards by the time we were released in 1979. It must be said that in prison our differences had become grotesque. I remember that some of the younger group – later to become leaders of the POCT – managed to pick up Radio Tirana at night on the little transistor radios we had, and would listen religiously to the nonsense that was broadcast. We would make fun of them, which of course inflamed tensions. They were 100 per-cent pro-Albanian communists, whereas we – the old guard

---

1. *Amel Tounsi* took the name of *Perspectives'* newspaper, meaning 'The Tunisian Worker' in Arabic. The movement started in 1971, and split from the founding members of *Perspectives* in 1973, becoming increasingly radical until it disbanded towards the end of the 1970s. Some of its members then created a new far-left movement called the *Parti ouvrier communiste tunisien*, POCT, still extant.

– had finished with all that long ago. It was then that I decided never again to work in politics with a capital P, but instead to fight for the defence of human rights. After the political and ideological break with *Amel Tounsi*, the first generation of *Perspectives* was thus intellectually ready to join the human rights movement from the mid-1970s on.

This evolution illustrates the capacity of the various components of the Tunisian opposition to come together again, no longer around a political programme, but in the wider defence of human rights. The Tunisian Human Rights League was founded in 1977 as a front uniting the political strands, no longer through partisan interest, but around the common denominator of the rights of the individual. People from different backgrounds took part in its creation – liberals from the urban bourgeoisie as well as intellectuals of the left. What is just as significant is that – from inside prison – former *Perspectives* members joined immediately, whereas members of *Amel Tounsi* did not.

There were six of us 'old' *Perspectives* members who backed the creation of the Tunisian Human Rights League. We were there, too, in 1981 during the first wave of repression against the Islamists, to denounce the trials brought against them for their opinions, while reaffirming our total disagreement with their way of thinking. The creation of the League at any rate marks a key date in the political life of the country insofar as learning the art of compromise may be seen as an essential feature of democracy.

Our development was accompanied, as elsewhere, by a profound disenchantment. Somewhere along the way we had lost the illusions of our youth. In this regard we were in tune with what was happening in Europe. We followed all the details of the errors of Maoism and the schisms of the revolutionary left. While Maria-Antonietta Macchiochi was still defending the Chinese Cultural Revolution, other writers denounced its misdeeds and spoke of different realities. The post-Stalinist regimes were largely discredited. More and more we listened to the dissident voices coming from the Eastern European countries.

Moreover, the fact that we had never responded to nationalist discourse or engaged in identity politics made it easier for us to subscribe to the universal values which underpin the struggle for human rights; that is to say, the fundamental recognition of the essential freedom and intrinsic value of all human beings. All this ultimately corresponded to our earlier internationalism, the feeling of being part of a global movement, a wider humanity beyond our local horizons. This implies a way of dealing with human relations based on the recognition of everyone's rights, provided they do not thereby exclude the rights of others, while taking into account their distinct identities.

Reaching out to the world

So it was that, when I left Tunisia in 1980, I joined Amnesty International, becoming a member of a local group that carried out certain tasks, such as writing letters for urgent actions and adopting prisoners of conscience. In April 1981, Simone and I helped found the Tunisian Section of Amnesty, its first branch in the Arab world. Its inaugural meeting was held in our apartment in Tunis, with police posted at the entrance to the building taking down people's names. These were mostly former political prisoners and their friends. On my release from prison in August 1979, I had stayed on in Tunisia until May 1980. During the first months I was placed under house arrest at home, near Gafsa. I remember the shock I got when I saw the wide open spaces of the rangelands once more after my long confinement in prison. Then, when I returned to Tunis, I got a job and very soon reintegrated into society. My wife returned regularly from Paris and we acquired an apartment.

I left Tunis for personal reasons and because I was drawn into the international mobilisation which had operated on my behalf. My wife, who is a French national although from a family that is Tunisian for many generations back, had a job in Paris, which made my decision easier. Besides, although banned from leaving the country since 1965, I obtained a passport very quickly during 1980. Some of my colleagues only managed to get theirs much later. International pressure had a lot to do with it. Pierre Mendès-France himself,[2] who remained close to Bourguiba, had at the time intervened to get me a passport. This was because the publication of my testimony in *Les Temps modernes* in April 1979 and its translation into several languages had made me widely known. Large extracts from it had been reprinted and made the headlines

---

2. Former French Prime Minister, 1954–55.

in Tunisian opposition newspapers such as *Erraï* and *Démocratie*. For all these reasons, international campaigns on behalf of our group had focused on me. So, in 1980 I left Tunisia for the first time in my life. I wanted to go out and see other places. It was a major step that I had refused to take while in hiding in 1972–73, when I could have left the country on false identity papers. That being said, although I went to live abroad, I never cut myself off from my country.

I also wanted to take part directly in the vast human rights movement that emerged worldwide at the end of the 1970s and beginning of the 1980s, in the incredible outburst of voluntary campaigning organisations which was the direct result of a general disaffection with politics. Up to the start of the eightie1980s, for instance, the International Federation of Human Rights (FIDH) existed, but under the protective wing of the French League for Human Rights. It was around this time that it began to expand until it eventually came to be more important than its parent body.

In essence, the movement to defend universal human rights may be seen as a last rampart against disengagement. One of the greatest challenges it faces today is the contest – in which it is one of the players – between universal and relative values. But this debate will never be settled, as the defence of individual freedoms will always pose a threat to the particular ways of different societies. The human rights movement will never escape this dilemma and will continue in an unsteady balancing act between, on the one hand, particularism and identity, and on the other, universality and internationalism. It is this pluralist tension which makes for the teeming variety of voluntary associations; their obligation is to act in the context of human diversity and social differences.

So these are the reasons, in all their complexity, that led me to join this movement. I wanted to contribute personally to the defence of prisoners of conscience, and to the defence of individual rights everywhere in the world, and I have done so. From 1980 to 1984, I lived in Paris and took up my economics studies again, while an active member of Amnesty International. I was also very busy looking after our son, born in 1981, as Simone was working. At that time I started travelling everywhere I had the opportunity to do so. It was in those years that I met the anti-apartheid militants in South Africa, and the defenders of the Helsinki agreements in Eastern Europe who, during the 1980s, were not yet free of their dictatorships.

In 1984, I went to live in London to work as Amnesty International's first co-ordinator of the movement's development in the Maghreb and the Middle East, including Israel. I lived there for six years. The task was daunting because the Arab human rights activists refused to meet the Israelis, not because they were opposed to the existence of human rights activists in Israel, but because such meetings could jeopardise them at home, where public opinion was fiercely anti-Zionist, almost anti-Jewish. When I arrived in an Arab country, I always told them that I worked with Israelis and that my wife was Jewish so that, right from the start, my position would be clear. It was only then that I had my first direct physical contact with the Arab world, which I had only known intellectually and whose poets and thinkers I had read. Now I was able to meet its intellectuals, writers, journalists and politicians in person. And several among them, such as the then Minister of Justice in Morocco, Omar Azziman, became members of Amnesty International.

My mission was a difficult one, consisting of setting up Amnesty sections and developing awareness of human rights in the Arab world, where it is still embryonic. For this issue was completely overtaken by the Palestinian question, with the focus of all political and intellectual elements of the Arab world homing in on it, coupled with a terrible mistrust of the West. The Arab world has turned in on itself in recent years and is suspicious of everything coming from the West, even if it eventually comes to accept it.

When I started work in the region, I met with a profound mistrust of Amnesty International, as a Western organisation that committed the greatest of sins in talking with Israel. For everything in this region is measured by the yardstick of the Palestinian issue. This was the context in which I had to convince people of the universality of human rights and of the need to defend them elsewhere than at home, as this is a basic principle of Amnesty's work. Moreover, this was still the time of the Cold War, and many human rights violations were the work of states – particularly socialist states – which supported the Arab world against Israel. How then could anyone criticise them?

I thus had to introduce the idea of the universality of rights to a region riddled with identity politics and focusing its resentment on its obsession with the Israeli-Palestinian abscess. And I had plans to mobilise the human rights defenders well beyond their own country and region... It is for all these reasons that, to this day, Amnesty International has never really managed to take root in the Arab world. The work of the FIDH is somewhat easier since its affiliates work primarily on human rights in their own countries. Amnesty International, on the other hand, requires its members to open up to the wider world beyond their own country.

In Jordan especially, where 60 per cent of the population is Palestinian, I crossed swords with militants who wouldn't work on anything except the violations of Palestinian rights by Israel. I was, moreover, accused of being a Mossad agent and had to bring a legal action for slander. Having moved over to human rights, I actually found myself once again in the middle of the eternal debate between nationalism and universal principles.

Defending the rights of all: the creation of PRI

In addition to the defence of prisoners of conscience, I was particularly interested in the world of prisons that I had got to know personally through the long period of my life spent in detention. From my time in prison I had started reading a whole body of literature about this world. My personal feelings and emotions had whetted my intellectual curiosity. I knew, for better or worse, the differences in treatment accorded to common-law and political prisoners. The former were sometimes better treated, but did not inspire the respect or fear that surrounded the latter. And I had been around ordinary prisoners enough to see how much they could be singled out for humiliation.

During my time in detention, I remember that once I was not far from a cell occupied by homosexuals. They had been put together in one of the cells on Death Row. They were young boys who earned a living from their bodies, wore makeup and gave themselves feminine names. And I witnessed the degradation, the abasement to which they were subjected solely on account of their sexual orientation. Yet within Amnesty, it was a long battle to secure the defence of such people, victims of discrimination by reason of their sexual orientation. Many Amnesty sections, especially those in the developing world, were reluctant to do so.

As a general rule, politicians everywhere, whether in power or in opposition, have scant concern for the violation of prisoners' rights. Even in 1999, when I was invited by Amnesty's Tunisian Section to talk about PRI, I heard a leading Tunisian opposition figure and former president of the LTDH (Tunisian Human Rights League) declare that, for the time being, dealing with common-law prisoners was a 'luxury'. Even today, the idea that defending ordinary prisoners is part and parcel of the struggle for human rights is not yet entirely accepted.

As part of my work at Amnesty, I had thus started to include prison conditions. In Sudan, for instance, during its brief democratic interlude from 1984 to 1989, several lawyers who were also members of Amnesty had decided of their own accord to offer legal aid to common-law prisoners. I gradually felt the need to work on prison conditions more generally and not just on prisoners of conscience, and so I started to speak about it to those around me. Among others, I discussed it with Vivien Stern, who at the time was Secretary-General of a leading British NGO, NACRO,[3] which deals with prisoners both in prison and after their release, and who later became one of the founders – with myself and others – of Penal Reform International (PRI). This organisation was thus born of the recognition that human rights organisations were not that much concerned with the humanisation of prison life. The coming together of people, ideas and experiences did the rest.

There were already quite a few national associations in Europe, such as NACRO or the Prison Reform Trust in the U.K., the Association of Prison Visitors, the Fédération de Soutien aux Déetenus or the Groupement étudiant national d'enseignement aux personnes incarcérées (GENEPI)[4] in France. In the United States, the American Civil Liberties Union already had a penal reform unit. The United Nations had an agency in Vienna for the prevention of crime and the treatment of offenders in Vienna, which later became the Centre for International Crime Prevention (CICP). But there was no non-governmental organisation at the international level catering for these issues. It was this common awareness of a few people, who at some point in their lives had

3. National Association for the Care and Resettlement of Offenders.
4. Prisoner Support Federation; National Student Group for the Education of Imprisoned Persons.

experienced the functioning of the criminal justice system, which brought them all together.

The core group of PRI's founders was composed partly by members of Amnesty International, myself included. The common denominator of all these people was their link with Amnesty International, either personally or as members. Vivien Stern, at the time married to the then Secretary-General of Amnesty, was a driving force for this meeting. Several associations, among them her own NACRO, and the Geneva-based Association for the Prevention of Torture, agreed to be founding members of PRI.

In November 1989, at the very moment the Berlin Wall came down – an event we heard about while in a working session – the inaugural meeting of PRI took place at the NACRO premises in London. Apart from Vivien Stern and myself, there were also members of several European, Latin American, Indian and African NGOs, as well as the former chair of Amnesty's International Executive Committee, Franca Sciuto. Without having planned it, the date was a very powerful symbol: we were founding PRI just at the very moment when one of the key totalitarian systems of the twentieth century was collapsing, and when the East-West divide was finally disappearing.

It was a strange time. The fall of the Berlin Wall, symbolic and spectacular as it was, occurred after a chain of events which had totally discredited the Soviet system. Our generation had already unmasked the falsehood on which it was built. So it was rather a sense of surprise that prevailed in November 1989: this system we had thought impregnable collapsed before our eyes like a house of cards. But we were pained too, because at the same time we were witnessing the triumph of something else that was far from convincing.

This key event did not usher in a truly liberal and democratic world, but rather a period full of contradictions, injustice and ugliness. What was more important to us at the time, however, was that we could now champion human rights without the ideological obstacles that had blocked our way before. The defence of these rights could at last become a truly universal vocation, even though we could already see that the West would not take long to find itself another enemy. In 1991, in an assessment of Amnesty's techniques, I had already touched on the issue of a 'new Satan' that the South in general and Islam in particular might represent for Westerners. The North-South divide was gradually taking over from the old East-West conflict.

North and South, a false dichotomy

In human rights terms, however, you can't really speak of a North-South divide. For while the form human rights violations take may change from one region to the next, the hard core of their defence is the same everywhere: respect for human dignity and for the common humanity of all people. I am one of those who believe in the universality of human rights, who think that humanity can free itself from prejudice, obscurantism and inequity, because human nature is the same the world over. Everywhere you find conflict between retrograde forces and those who yearn for progress. The United States is a good example of this: the worst type of violence can be found there, but also much that is good. So it is unfair to simplify the world using largely fictitious boundaries between North and South. There are aspects of the South in the North and of the North in the South. These are interwoven into the economies, the elites, the ideas and advances in thinking that go beyond the profound asymmetry that exists between two halves of the same world.

Take the example of the Muslim world, supposedly particularly opposed to abolition of the death penalty. The first Amnesty meeting there on this issue was held in Tunis in 1988. The previous year, a seminar on the same theme had been held in Pakistan. I took part in both. Progress was slow, but it was progress. An abolitionist association was set up in Tunisia in 2001 (though it was never legalised by the authorities). In the Lebanon, an abolitionist movement is also developing. In April 2000, the then Prime Minister, Selim Hoss, refused to sign the execution order for a man sentenced to death, declaring that it was against his personal convictions. Jordan was also the stage for debate on this issue. In 2001, when Palestinian courts condemned five men to death for allegedly collaborating with Israel, the director of prisons refused to witness the executions, saying he was against capital punishment. And don't let's forget that the fiercest resistance to abolition comes from the United States. In most Western countries, the majority of public opinion favours the death penalty, and governments have had to over-ride this factor to achieve abolition. In Muslim countries, those in favour of the death penalty base their case on religion, just as they do in order to justify the subordinate status of women. But it was not so very long ago that religious arguments of this nature became obsolete in the West.

Today, more than half the countries in the world, many of them in the Southern continents, have abolished the death penalty. This should encourage us to be optimistic, but nowhere is there linear progress, as we might like to believe. There may be steps backwards in some countries and then new steps forward. In the Philippines and several American states, the death penalty has been restored after abolition, and it is not impossible that a similar reversal may occur in South Africa. These are all reasons why the North-South divide is not necessarily an appropriate analogy, just as the religious argument is not pertinent either.

Much also depends on the degree of freedom enjoyed by NGOs and the material and financial resources at their disposal. At present, many of them depend on their Northern counterparts to be able to function, and even sometimes for their survival. Yet their credibility in the eyes of the local population is directly proportionate to their degree of autonomy. They should be able to build up this legitimacy within their own society by enhancing local capacity for thinking and acting upon all aspects of human rights work. Unfortunately, the lack of economic independence experienced by local human rights movements has important consequences for their aims, their work and their leadership. Those with clout in these associations are increasingly those who enjoy foreign support and are able to raise funds. Financial assistance from foreign NGOs, with the best will in the world, can sometimes damage the internal dynamics of local NGOs, and this may take long to rebuild.

We also need to recognise that such dependency is compounded by the repression that civil society is subject to in undemocratic countries. This obstructs its growth by preventing open debate, thereby preventing the NGOs from broadening their base. In these conditions, it is impossible for them to popularise any issues centred on human rights. Instead of working on what is essential, all their energy is spent on trying to raise funds abroad in order to pay the office rent, or for publications or travel costs. Travelling itself can become an income, which the NGO leaders share among themselves. This is how the lack of their own resources can lead NGOs astray from their more worthy goals.

But governments and foreign partners are not the only ones to blame for these impediments. They also illustrate the difficulty human rights associations have in rooting themselves in local soil. In many countries, political parties try to use them for their own ends, as a platform to speak out from, which they may not have in the strictly political field. As for governments, they may try to vindicate themselves or break up independent movements by creating their own NGOs, the so-called 'GONGOs'[5] which have proliferated in recent years.

Sometimes – but this is very rare – human rights NGOs in the South manage to collect funds locally. The Tunisian Human Rights League, for instance, has managed more than once to raise local funds for some of its activities or to ensure its defence. Tunisian artists have often been called upon to design their posters. It has organised major fundraising events; but this has only really been possible during the periods of liberalisation. During the 1980s, although it did not actually encourage them, the government left the human rights movements alone while the Islamists bore the brunt of official repression. For a while, this relative tolerance allowed companies and individuals to make donations to NGOs without being viewed as opponents of the regime and without their being bothered. All this seems like a dream compared to the nightmare that Tunisian human rights activists are going through nowadays.

All these problems were kept in mind when PRI was set up. It does not function through national or local sections, dependent on a central headquarters. When its resources allow, it creates regional offices and tries to respond as much as possible to local needs and realities. Usually these offices do their own fundraising and, except in a few cases, we don't create offices from scratch that are kept going by outside funding. Our donors are more often than not already involved in the region or interested by it, and it is they who request our assistance more than we do theirs. PRI's founders intended it to be a pragmatic and flexible organisation in order to have maximum effect. We don't go into a country on mission or for a consultancy and then leave, but instead we choose to work

5. 'Government-Owned NGOs'.

over the long term to help create the conditions for change, and always in partnership with local civil society and government departments, as this increases our chances of success. For change has to come about in the laws and the justice system, of course, but it also has to take root in people's minds and their culture.

In fact, in creating PRI we wanted to speed up the application of international norms and standards on prison management and the administration of justice, because prison is only part of a larger whole, this being the justice system and the way justice is delivered. The main objective of the courts should not be to put people in prison, but to ensure that justice is done. Most convicted persons should not be incarcerated: only those who represent a real danger to society or to themselves should be put in prison. This is why, from its inception, PRI has thought about and promoted alternatives to prison, such as mediation or community service. The idea of non-custodial sentences grew in strength during the 1990s. In 1990, the Eighth UN Congress on the Prevention of Crime and the Treatment of Offenders in Havana adopted the *UN Standard Minimum Rules for Non-Custodial Measures*. PRI, which was then about a year old, was present at this congress and contributed to the drafting of this text.

Since its inception, PRI thus chose to say No to local sections and Yes to programmes of action wherever possible, including through a regional presence. Thus our Moscow office, started in 1998, covers not only Russia, but all the other republics of the former Soviet Union. Our Costa Rica office covers the Caribbean and Latin America. In September 2001, we set up an office in Kathmandu for South Asia. We adopted this mode of organisation because PRI's founders believed that they should not try to reproduce Amnesty's system, which turned out to be very cumbersome to manage in spite of its extraordinary capacity for mobilisation. The other key difference is that we at PRI have favoured a professional approach: we depend on voluntary work, of course, but also on the input of experts and professionals.

Humanising prison

When we set up PRI we did not, of course, start off in a vacuum. During the 1970s, movements such as the *Groupe multi-professionnel de réflexion sur les prisons* (Inter-professional discussion group on prisons) were created in France. Foucault's writing about prison had set in train a new line of thought across Europe and North America. In the United States, the repression of the Black Panther movement and of anti-war protesters had also sparked off debate about the point of detention and the purpose of prisons, the dilemma between surveillance and punishment, on the one hand, and detention and rehabilitation, on the other. Pilot schemes working within and on prisons took place here and there, but for the most part they were still focusing on the situation of prisoners of conscience, such as the Vietnam War deserters or the Soledad Brothers. It is an inescapable fact that policy on imprisonment and detention advanced because of the existence of prisoners of conscience, from the time when fascism and Nazism were still present in Europe.

This is why the first steps towards humanising places of detention were taken after 1945. In Western Europe, some of the former resistance leaders who came to power had experienced prison and felt the need to create alternatives to the punitive custodial reflex. It was around this time that the idea began to take root that prison should not be a place of punishment but a context for rehabilitation and social reintegration. Then, during the 1960s and 1970s, some sociologists arrived at the idea that prison was incapable of rehabilitation but was a necessary evil. And if it is a necessary evil, we can't pretend it isn't there; it has to be dealt with since it is part of society.

According to this school of thought, prisons contain people who are criminals, but are at the same time both perpetrators and victims. Those who have committed crimes are of course serious offenders; but in this view, most are also victims condemned by society to commit criminal acts, by reason of their poor education, their social condition and their marginalised state. That is why society must assume responsibility for them. The question of prisoner rehabilitation is all the more acute in countries that have abolished the death penalty, which includes most of Europe, for most prisoners – including criminals – will leave prison at the end of a fairly lengthy sentence that counts as a repayment of their debt to society, and society cannot therefore simply wash its hands of them. Among other things, safety and security within the community depend on the successful reintegration of former prisoners.

At the beginning of the 1990s, other, much more radical theories sprang up, proposing that prisons be abolished altogether. They claimed not only that prison was not a solution, but that it also contributed to the criminalisation of society, acting as a school for crime. In the U.K., a government White Paper published in 1990 stated that prisons were little more than costly universities where already rotten individuals only learned to become worse. This is only partly true because many inmates are people whose guilt has never been, or not yet been, proven. Such is the case for the 50 to 70 per cent of the world's prison population who are remanded in custody awaiting trial, most of whom are in any case petty offenders. The scandal of their detention has fuelled criticism of the prison system as well as the claims that it is at best a necessary evil and at worst a useless or harmful institution.

Many specialists are reflecting on these issues nowadays. They debate them within international agencies and at UN conferences on the prevention of crime that have pushed forward the framework of international rules and standards for the treatment of prisoners. The rights of detainees have in fact been internationally recognised since the promulgation of the Universal Declaration of Human Rights, and upheld by the First UN Congress for the Prevention of Crime and the Treatment of Offenders in 1955.

This is where PRI comes in. In responding to a real need, the organisation has not only prompted interest from individuals and associations, but also from a growing number of states. Obviously this has not been achieved overnight. But quite early on, PRI started getting requests from governments needing assistance with their prisons, thereby widening its public constituency. The coherence and common stance of its founding group have also proved a crucial element in its success. This group is made up of mature people either with experience of prison and of human rights work, such as myself, or of working in prison and in the broader administration of justice. For some, this work was carried out in very large organisations, such as NACRO in the UK, which employs hundreds of staff and is funded mainly by government; others are criminologists, specialising in penal administration; still others are lawyers or sociologists.

And then, we did not want to go too fast and skip stages. It was only from 1996 on that PRI started its real development, recruiting more and more staff and opening a series of regional offices. Right from the start, however, it intended to play an international role. That's why its first large meeting was held in Tunis in 1991, in collaboration with the Tunisian Human Rights League and the Arab Institute of Human Rights, based in Tunis. Many Arab and African countries were present at this first meeting.[6] The second major conference took place in 1992 in Moscow. Then in 1996 we organised a Pan-African Conference in Kampala, Uganda, on prison conditions across Africa. In fact, it is all the detainees around the world that we are concerned about. That is how the adventure of PRI started off.

6. See *Penal Reform and Prison Reform*, report of an Afro-Arab seminar held in Tunis, 20 November–December 1991, published by the Arab Institute for Human Rights, Tunis.

3

CRIME AND PUNISHMENT

Before any prison sentence comes a court ruling. This is what needs to be looked at before considering the situation in prison.

The first question, even if it might at first seem incongruous, is whether the law is applied impartially and equitably to all those on trial. Does the court try actions, persons or situations? Does it hand down verdicts without prejudice? Real life shows, alas, that it doesn't. Judges are not super-humans removed from society and its prevailing ideas. Racial or religious minorities, women and the poor receive different treatment depending on which country they are tried in and what values are used to separate good from bad, licit from illicit acts.

The conditions by which justice is done are all the more alarming as, in general, judicial systems are desperately under-funded. Since governments are usually concerned with keeping justice on a tight rein, they tend not to grant it the budget needed for it to function independently of undue influence. There are too few judges and they are often poorly trained, especially in the South, where they are also underpaid. In such conditions, judges rarely correspond to the idealistic image that we sometimes have of them.

These shortcomings give a sombre impression of the way justice is rendered around the world. If some situations give rise to concern, there are nonetheless nuances. Not everything works in a uniformly bad way in the judicial world, and international standards are beginning to be applied almost everywhere, gaining

*ground progressively in regions where until recently they had been
ignored.*

*It is at any rate a good justice system that will provide reasonable
use of prison terms, defining the place of prison within the penal
system, and dethroning the custodial reflex from its dominant
position.*

Dispensing justice

The issue of judicial fairness has always been a matter for debate
in any organised society. The first rule of good justice lies in the
principle of separation of powers. It is imperative that the judiciary
should be independent of the executive and the legislature, the
latter making laws but not responsible for applying them. Good
justice also requires that everyone should be equal before the law.
These two elements lie at the heart of the concept of the rule of
law. To guarantee the independence and equity of the justice
system, it is vital that due process should obey no other rules than
those of justice itself: when any outside element intervenes, usually
either political or economic in character, independence and equity
are placed in jeopardy.

Now, in many countries, especially in the South, neither
independence nor fairness is guaranteed. Even in democratic
countries they are not always assured. The role of the Parquet
(public prosecutor's office) in France is a good example of this: you
can just see how the executive may be tempted to bend the rules in
matters of corruption involving institutions or persons close to
those in power. In totalitarian countries, by definition, political
control over the judiciary is total. And it has to be said that
nowhere in what is commonly called the Third World is justice
really independent, although there are big differences between
countries. In those with a longstanding democratic tradition, such
as India, the judiciary is relatively independent. In Egypt, it has
managed to retain a modicum of independence at the most
difficult times, when the totalitarian temptation was strongest for
those in power. There have even been instances when the State
Security Court has thrown out cases brought by the police. In
other countries, though, everything touching on the economic
interests of those in power escapes the long arm of the law.

Judges flouting the law and following orders from above are unfortunately very common in much of the world nowadays. At times, some of them rebel, as did the Tunisian judge Mokhtar Yahiaoui in 2001.[1] Everywhere, impartial justice has difficulty imposing itself once and for all, as the executive always proves tempted to exercise its control over the judiciary and is forever trying to encroach on its space. What differentiates countries from each other is how far the executive is actually able to do this and take control of the justice system. The world is, however, beginning to be aware of how important the independence of the judiciary is. The growing number of UN texts adopted by member states which thereby commit themselves to domesticating them into national law testifies to the fact that the demand for fair justice is beginning to be heard.

Impartiality is not an abstract notion. For the judiciary to be impartial, it needs not only to be independent from the executive, but also to have the will and the means to try cases without any outside interference. Furthermore, it must hand down its verdict within a reasonable time, taking into account the offence itself, the conditions in which it was committed, its effect on the victim(s) and the character of the offender. An impartial justice system does not simply apply the laws mechanically.

Delays in delivering justice are one of the most serious factors causing injustice: in some countries, as many as 70 per cent of detainees are on remand, awaiting trial. What is worse is that 60-70 per cent of them may have spent more time on remand than the sentence they would have received, as most detainees usually get less than six months. Here again, it would obviously be wrong to generalise. There are big differences, not only between countries, but also between the time in question and the cases themselves.

Only for the powerful...

Such delays are often due to the lack of effective co-ordination between the police, the judiciary and the prisons. Sometimes the prison services don't keep their files updated and fail to produce

---

1. On 6 July 2001, in an open letter to the President of the Republic, Moktar Yahiaoui denounced the compliance of the judiciary with executive orders and political abuse of due process. He lost his post.

the accused before the court. This kind of malfunction explains why detainees are sometimes quite literally forgotten in prison. Such delays result essentially from a lack of resources, training and political will.

The resources made available for justice and those it deals with are fundamental to the functioning of the criminal justice system and are essential for its impartiality. Throughout the world, justice systems lack resources, even in the old, rich democratic countries, where it remains a poor relation within government – to say nothing of countries with limited resources where even the most basic conditions of survival are barely met, where justice appears a luxury, and where judges are badly paid and socially undervalued by reason of their chosen calling. They are inadequately trained, and so they tend to leave the profession as soon as they can find employment elsewhere. Because they are few in number, there are long delays in reaching judgment and justice is thus denied.

In such countries, the accused are not judged by their alleged offence but on the basis of their economic situation and their social or political rank. And corruption here is all-pervasive. These shortcomings are all the more common where, as is often the case, states do not function through institutional logic, but through clans and clienteles, and for colossal financial stakes. In Colombia, as in other countries where drug cultivation and trafficking dominate the economy, the system of justice has been totally corrupted by drug traffickers, who hire the most prestigious lawyers and buy off judges. They thus obtain favourable rulings in total contempt of any sort of justice. Such practices are widespread in countries where the last few years have seen a big upsurge of organised crime.

In many less developed countries, judges and magistrates have not received any specific training. At best they have graduated from faculties of law. Some high-level judges may have trained in Western countries and others may at best have followed a course, but one too short to really train them. Very few countries have any school for judicial training. In poor regions, such as most of the African continent, regional training schools might have been envisaged but, unhappily, national pride has prevented such institutions being set up or, in the rare cases where they exist, have prevented them from developing. Nor is there any in-house training for judges.

The situation is even worse for certain categories of law-enforcement personnel, such as prison guards and the rest of the prison administration. In Africa, Senegal offers a modest training programme in this field, which sometimes takes in students from neighbouring countries. South Africa and Nigeria also have training structures for prison guards. Elsewhere on the continent, it is often the police or military who provide prison guards, just as they might be detailed to guard a bank or a ministry. The situation is no better in other regions. In Central Asia, Kazakhstan only opened a special school for prison guards in 2000. And as for court clerks, social workers and other categories of law-enforcement personnel, there is nothing. In some countries, the post of court clerk doesn't even exist. This dearth of training structures jeopardises the very functioning of the justice system.

Generally speaking, poor people run a greater risk of being convicted than do those with financial means or with connections in ruling circles. Not only do the poor have no money, but they also know next to nothing about the law, whether as offender or victim. This is what inequality before the law is all about, and it is a lot more common than you would think, since it doesn't just concern serious offences carrying prison terms. Inequalities also exist in civil cases, whether they involve payment of fines or surrender of property.

Frequently, poor people don't even have a lawyer. On a recent trip to Jordan, I found more than 1,000 inmates in a prison I visited. Out of eighteen people in one cell, all of them on remand, only one had a lawyer. In that country, the state is only obliged to provide legal aid for crimes punishable by death or life imprisonment. In other countries, the law prescribes legal aid for certain categories of remandees, such as minors. In many instances, the courts or the bar associations receive state funds to pay for legal aid in specific cases as required by law. Sometimes, bar associations also use their own resources to fund legal aid programmes for defendants in need.

Alongside this formal assistance, more and more NGOs provide legal aid for the most vulnerable categories of remand prisoners. Several PRI programmes include a legal aid component, as in Pakistan and Malawi, for instance. In Pakistan, local NGOs have formed a legal aid network of pro bono lawyers, which PRI is supporting. The government supports this project, which is easing congestion in courts and prisons by speeding up the prosecution and hearings of cases. In 1996, PRI initiated a legal aid programme for death row prisoners in the English-speaking Caribbean, enabling them to lodge appeals aimed at challenging their conviction or quashing their sentence, to petition for mercy, and to take their cases to the Inter-American Human Rights Court or to other regional or international mechanisms. Several convicted prisoners have won their appeals to these jurisdictions, by having their conviction struck down, or their sentence commuted. These legal victories created precedents resulting in new jurisprudence. Legal aid is thus a vital strategy for making justice more effective and impartial.

Parallel justice...

In many countries, however, things are more difficult because of the scarcity of courts and their distance from their clientele. Physical access to a judge then becomes very expensive. Studies in Zimbabwe, Bangladesh and India show entire regions without courts. And here, private or community jurisdictions take over. In Pakistan, the grand feudal overlords still occupy their traditional role as judges and even use their own private prisons. In other countries, certain types of offences never come before the formal courts but are dealt with by customary law mechanisms that are cheaper and closer to the people. The problem is that customary law is not always fair either. In India, for example, the caste system means that people from lower castes are heavily penalised. Generally speaking, women, lower castes and the poor rarely win cases under this type of jurisdiction. Customary law thus does not always ensure fairness, even if it affords quick and inexpensive judgment.

In the many countries which use customary law systems, offences may incur different penalties when they are handled by formal or traditional courts. I found one such example among the Mayas of Guatemala, where the community leaders dealt with the murderer of a family breadwinner whose crime was not referred to the public authorities: instead of imprisoning him or sentencing him to death, he was condemned to work the rest of his life to support the family of the dead man. This kind of sentence gives pause for thought, as it may well have a more positive effect than its statutory equivalent.

What is equitable justice? What is appropriate justice? It is quite difficult to answer these questions in the abstract; the context must always be taken into account. Culture and religion also influence the notion of what constitutes an offence. In some African countries, like Madagascar, cattle theft is an extremely serious crime punishable by death. In Nepal, it is a crime to kill a cow. In these countries, law is based on local culture, providing severe sanction for such acts. The same offence can thus receive quite different punishments depending on the country where it happens and the cultural context. The value of goods can also differ from one country to another: the theft of a bicycle is certainly more serious in China than in France. The most extreme case is Pakistan, where each year over 2,000 women are killed by their brother, father, husband or another male relative. When such cases come before the courts, they either go unpunished or receive only a light sentence because the judges show indulgence for such acts: in traditional culture, it is considered the family's duty to clear its honour by killing the woman, who is presumed guilty.

Certain acts of popular retribution can also only be explained by culture. Here, it is very difficult to draw the line between justice and vengeance. In so-called 'mob justice', you can't talk of justice in the formal sense, as a sovereign act carried out according to precise rules, but of the socially accepted punishment of a criminal act. The question that needs to be asked is why people have recourse to this kind of collective sanction.

When talking of justice, there are two types of norms: those that are explicitly recognised and those that are tacit. Both are situated outside the emotional field that characterises acts of revenge, which are punished by law. Nonetheless, the line between justice and vengeance is sometimes blurred. In some cultures, it is the latter that is codified. This is the case even now in Jordan or the Yemen. But being codified does not necessarily transform revenge into justice. There are also cases where self-styled Robin Hoods contest legal justice to impose their own. An example was in Benin, where judges and police had to leave a locality after being threatened by a local 'enforcer' – who was very popular, by the way – because they had failed to issue verdicts and impose sentences that conformed with the norms of the rural community, who considered the man a hero and protected him. The authorities knew quite well where he was, but his enormous popularity guaranteed him immunity.

So again, why are these practices becoming widespread in countries which for some time now have had a formal legal framework? Why has the lynching of petty thieves become so common in big African cities? As for the police in charge of law and order, more often than not they don't intervene, either because they condone mob justice, or because they are afraid of the mob, which could as well turn on them. The main reason for the fresh upsurge of mob justice is, in my view, due to the fact that people have little or no trust in the formal justice system in their country.

...or alternative justice?

While there is still need for caution, we can explore the solutions which so-called informal justice may offer. In a number of countries, attention is now being paid to individuals and groups who can make an original contribution to conflict resolution within communities. It is also of note that many countries in transition or upheaval owing to civil conflict see informal conflict-resolution mechanisms being set up. In South Africa during the anti-apartheid struggle, in Mozambique during the war against the Portuguese colonial power, in Uganda under the regimes of Idi Amin Dada and Obote-II, local people used parallel judicial procedures.

Some governments tried to make these systems permanent by reinstating justices of the peace or by creating courts with a single judge. PRI got interested in these experiments and in 1999 set up an Access to Justice programme which tries to promote new models of justice and penal administration in developing countries, mainly in India, Bangladesh and some African and Caribbean countries. It first involves first studying existing efforts, and then helping those who invest in them, usually NGOs. The idea is to try and promote alternative judicial procedures while improving traditional methods, which, as we have seen, are often biased in favour of dominant groups or patriarchy.

In Bangladesh, for example, PRI is trying to widen the circle of people able to dispense traditional justice. Women are being trained, among others, so that they can take part in the process of conflict mediation. In Rwanda, by reason of the genocide, the exodus that followed it and the imprisonment of tens of thousands of adult men, whole communities are now almost entirely made up of women, in a country where the judicial system has been virtually destroyed. The women have come together in committees to rule on local conflicts, thus reviving the tradition of *gacaca*, or popular grassroots justice. In doing so, they have taken on a role that was formerly confined to men. Here is an interesting example on which we are working to find fair solutions in situations where there is no functioning rule of law.

A diverse situation worldwide

Although we might conclude from this that the situation worldwide is not particularly good, this impression needs to be nuanced and certain situations given a historical or contextual explanation. The most extreme example at the start of the twenty-first century is that of Rwanda. Out of a population of 7 million, this country has some 120,000 to 130,000 prisoners detained since the 1994 genocide, most of them still awaiting trial.[2] Burundi is in a very difficult situation: 90 per cent of the detainees in Bujumbura's central prison are awaiting trial. But there are other countries which bring people to trial more quickly and more effectively, and where the proportion of remandees may be no more than a quarter of the prison population. The world average, as we have seen, varies between 50 and 60 per cent.

This figure reveals how poorly the worldwide functioning of the justice system is faring, and that is without counting China, where statistics are either unreliable or non-existent. The countries that fare least badly are those where society does not produce high crime rates, where the laws are not too harsh and where necessary attention is paid to the administration of justice. So we should not lose hope, especially as many states have come to realise how vast the problem is and are attempting to improve their judicial systems by, among other things, appealing to organisations such as PRI.

These are, above all, countries undergoing a transition to more open and democratic societies where there is the political will to change things. This drive for improvement first showed itself in a number of Latin American countries emerging from dictatorship. For several years now, this has also been the case in the Central

2. Figures for 2002.

and Eastern European countries. Several sub-Saharan African
countries are also beginning to move. Some of them, notably post-
apartheid South Africa, are in the forefront of the reform
movement.

But the change is also to be seen in poorer countries, such as
Mali. Every year since 1993, the authorities there have held a
forum for democratic debate on 10 December, Human Rights Day,
where anybody can come and complain about the public services
and civil servants. In 1999, a national forum on the administration
of justice was held, after over a year of preparations. This took the
form of a national consultation in the capital, Bamako, where the
main problems facing the country's justice system were laid out
and debated.

The Arab world is more gingerly engaging with the reform
process. Jordan and Morocco are making laudable efforts in this
direction. At the beginning of 2001, Jordan reduced the legal limits
of police custody, and the length of time for remand was limited
and strictly regulated. In Lebanon, a new code of criminal
procedure adopted in 2001 opened up interesting prospects by
decriminalising several types of behaviour formerly considered
offences. For instance, homosexuality, though not entirely
decriminalised, is no longer punishable by imprisonment. In order
to reduce acute overcrowding in prison, the new Lebanese code
also decreed that anyone sentenced to less than a year in prison
could receive a suspended or other non-custodial sentence. This
country has thus chosen to reduce the use of prison terms for
minor offences. These are concrete steps that give grounds for
optimism.

Justice and prison

Having said this, imprisonment may still be seen as a step forward
compared to some punishments commonly used in the past, such
as banishment, corporal punishment or the death penalty, which is
still widely applied. Prison has historically represented an
alternative to other, more barbaric, punishments. Moreover,
detention has been made more humane since 1945, thanks to the
UN Charter and Universal Declaration of Human Rights. The
Geneva Conventions on international conflict also stand as
essential texts. In 1955, the United Nations established rules for

the treatment of prisoners.[3] In 1966, it dealt with juvenile crime and the treatment of minors. For some years now, the UN has taken a further step in preparing and submitting international texts on organised transnational crime and traffic in human beings.[4] This array of standards, agreed in principle by the international community, is likely to be further elaborated in coming years. Nevertheless, although these developments are in many ways positive compared to past practices, privation of liberty has become the norm as the sanction of choice.

Since the 1950s, however, the legitimacy of prison as a system of punishment, and its efficacy, have been called into question. Paradoxically, it is often prison authorities who question its effectiveness and thereby challenge the whole system of imprisonment as such. They are best placed to see that prisons are used by society for indiscriminately ridding itself of misfits – for some countries still detain people for vagrancy or other types of socially harmless behaviour, such as not having identity papers. This means that prison authorities are often the most determined proponents of a more measured use of a prison system that should not be an instrument of social control.

As a general rule, imprisonment is justified for those violent criminals who are a danger to society. This is the real norm. It can also be justified if it serves to protect an offender who might be at risk if released. But this need should not become a pretext for imprisonment, as is increasingly the case. In Bangladesh, Pakistan and Jordan, for example, women who have 'dishonoured' the family are increasingly put behind bars. The state clearly has a duty to protect them against clan reprisals, but, in reality, they find themselves treated as the guilty party, as if they were the ones who had really committed the offence. The state deprives them of freedom instead of giving them proper protection and working to change the prevailing mentality.

Detention should therefore only be resorted to within a framework of fair and equal rules, and only to protect society from violence. In no circumstances should it be used as a way of managing transgression and social differences, by removing from

---

3. UN Standard Minimum Rules for the Treatment of Prisoners, 1955.
4. Notably the UN Convention on Transnational Organised Crime (2000) and the Palermo Protocol.

circulation all those who represent a problem to society, which is, after all, nothing more than a modern form of banishment. Nowadays, delinquents and misfits are hidden away as if they no longer exist, and are thus condemned to a social death.

Prisons are, moreover, all too frequently used as an instrument of political control. Justice is then used as a means to eliminate political opponents. In 2001, the Chadian government arrested all presidential candidates standing against the incumbent between the two rounds of the presidential election. Detention can in this way become a tool of dictatorships and indeed a way of exercising power.

Prison should therefore be given a positive role, which is clearly not the case when it aims to place human beings out of sight and out of mind. Privation of liberty should involve treatment, since the prisoner is considered abnormal by reason of transgressing current social norms. All detainees should then benefit from being taught how to live in society again. This approach is totally at odds with certain lines of thought, notably American beliefs that attribute criminality to genetic factors. Still, a policy of rehabilitation and social reinsertion of prisoners can only really work within a more general policy framework that decriminalises many offences and abandons the penal custodial reflex. To benefit from such programmes, the affected population should be reduced to the absolute minimum of those who pose a real danger to society. With a smaller prison population and more resources, you can begin to reduce re-offending and the contagion of criminality by confinement.

Prison should, lastly, exercise a protective function rather than serve as punishment. Privation of liberty should be the only punishment, and not poor conditions of detention as well. Apart from this deprivation, all other human rights should be guaranteed the prisoner. Respect of those rights is, moreover, a precondition for any rehabilitation programme. It should always be borne in mind that virtually all those who enter prison are supposed to leave it one day. It is because this basic precept is far too often forgotten that prisons throughout the world serve as schools for regressive behaviour.

4

PRISONS – A WORLD APART

⁓⁓❦⁓⁓

Contemporary societies want more prisons. Over a few decades, punishment by imprisonment has become – in peoples' minds – a universal panacea for all forms of delinquency, including the most harmless. This belief that 'prison works' has led today's world to rush into an exclusively custodial reflex with what are in many ways disastrous consequences.

In spite of studies showing that the heaviest sentences have no deterrent effect, nothing seems able to change this mindset. With a few rare exceptions, judges nowadays hand down prison sentences more often and more harshly. In the last quarter-century, the prison population has increased nearly everywhere in the world at a much faster rate than the population in general. The United States, world leader in the field, has seen its own prison population quadruple since 1980, while the crime rate has increased by only 7 per cent. In 2001, the world's only super-power had more than 2 million detainees, compared to just under 1.3 million in 1992 and around 500,000 in 1980. With 669 prisoners per 100,000 inhabitants, the United States is roughly on a par with Russia, where the number of prisoners went up from some 722,000 in 1992 to over a million in 1998. The total number of Russians decreased slightly from 148 to 146 million between 1990 and 2000, thus achieving a ratio of 680 per 100,000, a figure which has since dropped somewhat. Compared to these two countries, China seems almost virtuous with – as far as we know – 115 prisoners per 100,000 inhabitants and a total number of detainees officially estimated at 1.5 million.[1]

The full consequences of this rush to imprisonment on the health and social and psychological well-being of detainees have yet to be established. With regard to prisoners' health, the statistics are downright catastrophic in some countries. Everywhere, rates of morbidity and mortality for detainees are much higher than the national averages. Tuberculosis and AIDS are devastating prisons the world over. In African prisons, the prevalence of tuberculosis has reached 665 per 100,000, compared to 60 per 100,000 for the rest of the population.[2] In 2000, nearly 100,000 Russian prisoners, roughly 10 per cent of the prison population, had tuberculosis, and more than 4,000 had AIDS. In Brazil, 20 per cent of detainees are HIV-positive. In Puerto Rico, 94 per cent of detainees have Hepatitis C, according to the Atlanta Center for Disease Control. I could go on for much longer with this tedious litany of horror.

The custodial reflex therefore does not solve anything – quite the contrary. This option does not, however, appear to be receding, as a collective obsession with security seems to be a characteristic of contemporary society in both the northern and southern hemispheres.

Overcrowding in prisons

The world prison population is approaching 9 million individuals. This figure – given by the United Nations – is approximate, insofar as we do not know the exact number of detainees in China. But, as each detainee is part of a family, the number of people directly affected by prison is much higher: at least triple the number of detainees. Another feature is that the overwhelming majority of the prison population is male, essentially young adult males in the prime of life. This aggravates the problems caused by promiscuity. Sexuality

1. Statistics about numbers of detainees vary. For the U.S.A. figures are those given by the International Centre for Prison Studies and the website *www.prisonactivist.org*; the figures for Russia and China come from *www.prison.org*.
2. International Conference on HIV/AIDS in Prison in Africa, 16–18 February 1998, Dakar.

is a major problem in the prison context, and promiscuity means that the prison environment is also very pathogenic, with young prisoners exposed to all sorts of contagious diseases. Tuberculosis, for instance, takes on catastrophic dimensions and affects tens of thousands of people in many countries. The danger that such a situation presents for public health is almost never taken into account.

Depending on the country, women represent only 2 to 5 per cent of this population. As they are more rarely engaged in the public economic domain than men, with fewer public responsibilities and less power, they are less prone to corruption. They also go out less often in public and as a result are somewhat sheltered from committing certain offences. Besides, society no doubt protects women more than men. Their status has, in some ways, two sides to it: in male-dominated societies they are given less power and fewer responsibilities, as they are considered the weaker sex, in need of protection and deserving pity, at the same level as other categories of so-called vulnerable persons. And lastly, there are certain types of crime, such as rape, which are specific to men. But, paradoxically, women commit more serious crimes than petty offences. Many women have been convicted for the murder of the man in their life. In 1992, the women's prison in Tirana, Albania, held twenty-five women detainees, all of them convicted for murdering their husband, father or brother. Often, women have no choice other than suicide and murder. In Pakistan, Iran and all other sexually repressive societies, you find an abnormally high suicide rate among women.

Measured in terms of their holding capacity, prison overcrowding is a feature common to all countries in the world, with very few exceptions. A prison's accommodation capacity is not calculated only by the number of beds. It must take into account other vital facilities such as kitchens, toilets, showers, refectories, meeting rooms, recreational and sports facilities. You can also measure overcrowding by the ratio of detainees per 100,000 inhabitants. Worldwide, this varies from around 700 per 100,000 in the United States and Russia, which hold the records for excessive prison use – setting aside the extreme situation in Rwanda – to a minimum of around 100 to 150 per 100,000, to be found mostly in Western Europe. Scandinavian countries have for a long time had the lowest imprisonment ratios.

Over the last quarter-century, the number of prisoners worldwide has soared. This is because public opinion everywhere clamours for imprisonment as a miracle solution to crime. The

world today demands ever more prison. This trend is increased by
two mutually reinforcing phenomena: the role of the media and
the rhetoric employed by politicians in democratic countries.

'Less prison' is certainly not an election winner these days. The
fight against crime and the need to strengthen security, on the
other hand, reap dividends with a public that needs reassuring.
Everything is done as though politicians are only responding to the
supposed demands of public opinion, whose fears they have
played upon, thereby anticipating its demands. Election strategies
are developed on the basis of what can make a candidate popular,
and achieving popularity is often seen by the strategists as
satisfying the demand for security, well ahead of other equally
crucial issues such as employment. It's as if, in each election
campaign, the most conservative element of the electorate needs to
be mollified by pandering to its demands. And these issues are
magnified by the coverage they get in the media. This is how the
demand for security above all else is created, and where foreigners
often pay the price first. In their defence, it must be said that
stigmatisation of immigrants is not the sole prerogative of rich
countries. You can find it everywhere, notably in Africa and the
Middle East. During the French election campaign of 2002,
politicians took this populist approach to security to extremes
bordering on caricature.

The role of the media is key to forming public opinion. The
prime objective of most of them is to sell newsprint, and to do this
they favour sensational items. Following the politicians' lead, they
assume the public is avid for this kind of information, which
provides fertile soil for security concerns. And, as it is held that
'zero tolerance' is the best guarantee of public security, that does
the trick.

This belief that 'prison works' comes from the false conviction
that there is a deterrent effect on the offender. Yet many studies
show that there is no causal relation between committing the
offence and fear of punishment. A criminal does not think before
committing a murder of the punishment he will incur. The United
States provides a real caricature of this erroneous way of thinking.
What is terrifying about it is that, in spite of a drop in petty crime
in recent years, politicians are demanding an even greater use of
prison. There was the case of a man sentenced to twenty-five years
in prison for stealing a slice of pizza, by virtue of the 'three strikes'
rule, which requires that after three offences, however serious or

trivial the offence, a repeat offender is automatically condemned to twenty-five years with no remission.

The United States, Russia and their emulators

A quarter of the world's prison population, just over 2 million people, is in the United States, although it has only 4 per cent of the global population. This situation can be explained in large part by the country's violent history and its cult of individualism. The most striking example of this heritage is the – to me – unbelievable way it handles the firearms issue. Here is a country where children are brought up knowing how to use guns, without any thought for the potentially catastrophic consequences of such familiarity. Each time an attempt is made to tackle this problem, there are always people to be found invoking the sacrosanct freedom of the individual to defend himself and to decide what is good for him. Their particular heritage also helps to explain why the American justice system is blatantly racist, with 'people of colour', although a minority in the population at large, being abnormally over-represented within the prison population.

Besides this, the marriage of individualism and economic liberalism that characterises the United States means that everything is considered in terms of money. The private sector is seen as synonymous with efficiency, so that even the administration of justice is now being privatised, with many prisons going into private management. These private prisons are not even required to respect the terms of their contracts, while the companies that manage them are listed on the Stock Exchange. The greater the number of beds filled in their prisons, the higher the value of their shares. In a country where the art of lobbying has reached a degree of near perfection, there is a danger that the prison lobby will do its utmost to accentuate the punitive reflexes of the justice system.

The United States possesses a 'crime economy' stretching from organised crime and mafias all the way to the justice system itself. Handling crime is a business activity. Negative trends in the justice and prison systems reveal the extent of the crisis American democracy is going through today: for the state of a nation's prisons is a good indicator of the health and level of its civilisation. The crisis in the American justice system is thus a manifestation of a crisis of values. The state, which has theoretically removed the individual's right to exercise justice by arrogating the monopoly of justice to itself and placing it above particular interests, is now relinquishing that monopoly to private groups and individuals for money.

Australia has a prison management system rather similar to that of the United States. Some other countries have even gone further with regard to aspects of prison management, but in different forms. Thus, France has for a long time contracted out catering, education and training to the private sector, but not surveillance – the authorities have not privatised prison management itself. The United Kingdom also has private prisons: the Home Office has allowed competition between the public and private sectors here, based on precise conditions of contract. According to the authorities, this competition has improved public sector functioning and has resulted in more humane prison conditions.

But the real threat nowadays are the multinational companies – whether British, American or French – that specialise in prison management and compete with each other to sell their know-how to the developing world. A British company has pressed Malawi and Lesotho into signing a contract. A French company is in negotiations with the Lebanese government. Another company, American this time, has built the biggest prison in South Africa. The danger is appreciable when you bear in mind that most developing countries have no way of controlling this situation and that corruption is endemic to them. So it is a tempting solution for countries devoid of means when they are offered both the construction and management of prisons, without having to spend any money.

Russia is another caricature of the custodial culture and illustrates how all countries undergoing 'transition' can be blown off course. When we talk of transition in the former socialist countries, we usually think in terms of democracy; but it is also a transition towards an economic free-for-all that provokes great economic insecurity and soaring unemployment. (And this, incidentally, is one of the reasons why communist parties are being voted back into power quite democratically in some of these countries.) It is a context which allows economic crime to really take off. Mafias have proliferated and the *nouveaux riches* flaunt their opulence quite brazenly. Those in power also use the excuse of economic crimes to bring the opposition to heel. Beneath all this, part of the impoverished population employs any means they can to survive, while the informal sector has grown enormously. This conjugation of circumstances explains the appearance of new forms of criminality.

Moreover, the prison system itself has gone into crisis. Under the Soviet model, prisons were integrated into the planned production economy, which has now been destroyed. So nobody knows how to run the prisons any more, now that they no longer bring in any revenue. The buildings are left unmaintained and prisoners are left to their own devices. This being said, Russia is doing what it can to fight prison overcrowding. To this end, it has voted several amnesty laws, one of which, in 2001, resulted in the release of more than 100,000 prisoners.

Old and new offences

The American and Russian cases are all the more worrying in view of the many studies that have shown that the crime rate has not increased in countries which have abolished the death penalty or reduced the use of prison. But public opinion is rarely influenced by real statistics; it usually reacts to other, much more emotive stimuli.

Besides, statistics can show an increase in certain offences simply because they are being reported more often. This is the case with sex crimes and especially with sexual abuse of children. That being said, we should be glad that some acts are now considered offences punishable by imprisonment. Rape, in the past considered a minor offence, is now seen as a crime in a growing number of countries. In some countries, such as Tanzania, it incurs a mandatory prison term, which the judge does not have the right to reduce. Conversely, some acts which constituted an offence in the past are now considered normal, or at any rate acceptable. Evolving technology has also created new offences, such as computer crime. Finally, the spectacular growth of organised crime over little more than a decade, thanks among other things to improved communications technology, has prompted an increase in prison sentences.

More generally, in today's world we are witnessing a growing criminalisation of offences and the constant intrusion of justice into new areas. For instance, the domain of the family is confronted much more than before by ever more frequent prosecutions for domestic violence or incest. Conversely, the shortcomings of some state authorities are such that the justice system can handle only a small proportion of the work that falls within its jurisdiction. A 1996 University of Lagos survey showed that 86 per cent of offences committed in Nigeria are not even reported to the police. Studies in the U.K. have shown that, out of a hundred socially harmful individuals, only seven will ever actually go to prison. Such figures need to be divulged in order to convince people that the custodial reflex is not a solution. Imprisonment should remain a last resort for it to preserve its full meaning as a solution. It is a necessary form of protection and a way of managing deviant behaviour that should be used advisedly. Above all, we should understand that the perception of insecurity is not always a true picture of reality.

Today's living conditions, above all in the world's mega-cities where social ties are loosened, also play a part in increasing what we might call security-related stress. The inhabitants of these cities don't know each other, or trust each other; they can't rely on each other, and don't feel protected by their neighbourhood. The very idea of neighbourliness has practically disappeared, replaced by a barricade mentality. As people are no longer neighbours, they protect themselves with technical devices – alarm systems have never sold so well. This development encourages crime because as people no longer feel the need to respect social codes, and because the mutual surveillance that went with living close together can no longer be practised. In traditional communities, crimes are less common because this mutual surveillance acts as a collective constraint on individuals.

Town planning can, according to how it is done, prove a factor in increasing as well as reducing crime. Sociological studies carried out in South Africa have found that when a road is built around the periphery of a town instead of through its centre, delinquency is reduced. It has also been shown that when a district has no green spaces, no place for young people to meet, no communal meeting-place, and where there is no contact between generations, young people are left to their own devices and make up for this by congregating in gangs and clans.

Added to this, society collectively stigmatises the inhabitants of problem suburbs, which are often cut off from the rest of town. This only increases the feelings of exclusion and frustration, and hence the desire for social revenge, which grip many of those living there. The way cities are built therefore contributes to the disintegration of the social fabric, which in turn, for those already on the borderline, undermines their fragile capacity to distinguish between right and wrong.

A crisis of criminal justice

Various elements can thus explain the knee-jerk reaction of politicians and legislators in so many countries in resorting to the excessive use of prison and increasingly tough law-making. They feel that they should be responding to popular expectations by showing themselves to be ever more repressive. Whenever a murder is committed by a recidivist or by a prisoner on day-release near the end of his sentence, the justice system is immediately accused of being lax and people start demanding greater strictness. This is also probably why politicians pay so little attention to crime prevention.

This demand for instant fixes also prevents the justice system from doing its work. It is overwhelmed by the ever-growing number of cases it has to handle. The system is creaking under its own weight and the resources to deal with the increased load are not always available, while the physical infrastructure is deteriorating. Periods spent on remand grow ever longer and court cases take up more and more time, which in some countries paves the way for corruption, as you have to pay for your case to get an early hearing. Justice is thus diverted from its true calling and is delivered in an ever more arbitrary and unfair manner. This situation heightens people's loss of trust in the justice system, which in turn encourages them to take justice into their own hands, in a reversion to non-state, communal forms of justice. This is how the crisis is deepening within the criminal justice systems of even the most developed countries.

In the developing countries of the South, this crisis is dramatic. And when some of their authorities declare their wish to improve the system, all they do is raise the prison walls higher and multiply the number of watchtowers. This is what prison reform means, more often than not. And in the meantime, the prisoners are left to themselves in often atrocious conditions, such as those I saw in the Lebanese prison where prisoners have to sleep in the latrines for lack of space. Some governments do want to find a solution, such as those southern and eastern countries in transition, but they lack the means to do so, and the international community does not help them much. It appears to be more interested in fighting transnational organised crime than in reforming the administration of justice.

Sometimes, prisoners rise up against delays in judicial procedures. In Niger in 1998, I heard from the senior prison managers themselves the tragic story of a group of rebellious prisoners. They had refused to go to court, arguing that their cases would not be heard anyway, since only important people enjoyed the privilege of an early trial. In the course of the altercation, they manhandled the prison director a bit. The Republican Guard, charged with putting down this revolt, locked the twenty-nine ringleaders in a cell over the weekend pending their transfer to a prison in the desert. The detainees began to suffocate without any ventilation in their overcrowded cell. To quieten them down, the guards lobbed in some teargas grenades, and all of them died. This is how prisoners can end up, when they may have committed only petty offences but cannot bear to wait any longer for their trial. A good many of them would probably have been released at the end of their trial anyway.

Prison overcrowding is generally catastrophic in the countries of the South. Since these countries do not usually have the means to handle overcrowding, the treatment of most detainees contravenes the most elementary rules of respect for individual rights. Where there is no prison administration, the police – who generally manage security – designate certain prisoners to act as guards and to maintain order, with the attendant disruption that you can imagine. In 1994, there were no prison guards in the central prison of Kathmandu. The prisoners who assumed this function even had a uniform and a truncheon; their boss, who was a prisoner himself, had 104 men under his command! In Rwanda, where there is admittedly a rather unusual situation, the prisoners responsible for overseeing the other inmates wear a cap with the word 'Security' printed on it. Such situations are all the more serious in that it is gangster bosses who are usually chosen to keep order. And even when the prisoner-warders do not start out as bosses, they turn into them in any case, by reason of the power they are given over others, as they are the ones who organise life in prison, distributing water and food, deciding on rewards and punishments.

As for living conditions for the prisoners, they are horrendous in many poor countries. In Pakistan, the authorities spend only 25

U.S. cents a day per detainee, and in some cases even less. But if this derisory sum is multiplied by the number of inmates in Pakistani prisons – 80,000 – you realise that it represents a significant daily charge on the state budget. The custodial reflex therefore costs a lot of money to maintain for countries that nonetheless find it impossible to satisfy the most basic needs of the prison population.

Dramatic health and social problems

The world's prison population is made up for the most part, as we have seen, of poor young adult males. Now, these prisoners are frequently family breadwinners, and their families suddenly find themselves deprived of an important part, if not their only, source of income, while the children are often the most affected. In Rwanda, where the prison population is abnormally high, women find it hard to deal with work in the fields on their own, and their production feels the pinch. Not only does the prisoner stop bringing food home; he also becomes a burden when the family has to supply him regularly with food supplements. The families of detainees thus grow more vulnerable and tend to get even poorer. They can also be ostracised by their community and excluded from communal activities. Family breakdown caused by the imprisonment of a family member can thus go very far, even reproducing criminal tendencies among the younger generation.

Add to this the risk to public health. A Zambian judge once gave me an example of the folly of the custodial reflex, in a case that she herself had had to deal with. She had sentenced a young accountant to six months in prison for embezzlement. After being raped by other inmates, the young man died of AIDS before the end of his sentence. This judge could not get over her feelings of guilt, having unwittingly condemned to death a man who was guilty, not of a crime but of a petty offence. This unhappy story serves to illustrate how dramatic the problems of health in prison can be. This is why, at PRI, we call for health in prisons to be the preserve of the Ministry of Health and not the prison authorities. Public health should not, in fact, be managed by an administrative structure whose primary aim is repression. Some countries have taken this step, and not only in the wealthy democracies. In Jordan and Senegal, health in prisons falls under the responsibility of the

Ministry of Health. Each department should deal with what lies within its competence, and health is no exception to this rule, just as professional training or education is not the business of the prison management, but that of the ministries and departments which have the necessary competence to deal with them.

Halting the mindless reaction

Many people are calling nowadays for the decriminalisation of some offences, which would reduce the prison population. But even without considering non-custodial alternatives, such a reduction can already be achieved by more intelligent management of the prison population, first of all by separating prisoners into different categories. This would limit the use of high security prisons, which require large sums of money, to people who represent a real danger to society. Once serious criminals are thus isolated, we could have open or semi-open prisons, which need less surveillance and thus smaller budgets. The internationally agreed rules recommend this 'categorisation' of prisoners, considering it a prerequisite for good prison management practice.

All prison managers should therefore make a preliminary case-study of each detainee on arrival to assess their state of health, their needs, educational level and professional qualifications, their psychological traits and the risks they represent. Depending of course on the offence or crime committed, and also on the detainee's age, they would create profiles for the purpose of managing each detainee personally. Based on this preliminary work, they could create groups of detainees and place them within different prison regimes. There are violent, often recidivist, prisoners with serious psychological problems who need placing in special facilities. During detention, a prisoner may also undergo crises that render him temporarily violent or dangerous, and which require special treatment. Only categorisation can enable a country to know what its real needs are for high security prisons.

Some countries are already making efforts to reduce their prison population. In Lebanon, for instance, prisoners with good behaviour get an automatic reduction of three months per year of their sentence. In Zambia, open prisons have been in existence for several years. I visited a small agricultural prison there whose boundary was marked only by ropes and pickets, with no guards around. It is run by prisoners near the end of their sentences who have shown good behaviour during their detention and shown they have no intention of escaping. They cultivate plots of land, not only for their own needs, but also for sale. In this way, the prison can be self-supporting and the work teams manage themselves: the prisoners go to the fields and return without any overseer. Even the trucks transporting the produce are driven by detainees. This experience shows that prison conditions can change at successive stages of the sentence, according to the category of prisoner. The Zambian prison commissioner made a presentation of this prison farm model to the United Nations in 2000, at a meeting organised by PRI.

Cramming all prisoners together in high security blocks is an aberration, without counting the waste of resources that this mistaken course of action implies. A Tunisian proverb says that if a mouse falls into a jar of oil, then all the oil is spoilt. The same could be said of prisons: if all the prisoners are mixed together – as is too often the case – putting a cheque fraudster side by side with a murderer or an armed robber, the worst criminals will contaminate all the others in the group. It is cohabitation with hardened criminals that creates a school for crime.

5

PRISON – A CARICATURE OF SOCIETY

How does one survive in prison? Nearly everywhere in the world, there is a sort of conspiracy of silence about the conditions of prison life, which public opinion is not much concerned about. It requires a dramatic event, such as a mutiny, a hunger- strike or an imprisoned celebrity, for the world of prisons to be remembered now and again by 'normal' people. Although prison is a daily ordeal for all prisoners, it is even more so for the most vulnerable among them, lacking the means to defend themselves in this closed environment, which is hidden from the eyes of the outside world and dominated by violence and misery, even in rich and democratic nations.

PRI is not a prison watch organisation, nor does it denounce prison conditions. Its members do, though, visit prisons systematically to ascertain what state they are in, their needs and what could be improved. Generally, it is parliamentarians or representatives of official bodies who are mandated to report on conditions of detention in a country. International organisations such as the International Committee of the Red Cross (ICRC) or the Committee for the Prevention of Torture (CPT) in Europe, as well as the United Nations Special Rapporteurs, carry out this work. These public figures or institutions intervene according to a set of strict rules. They must, among other things, be able to select the prison they want to visit, so that a government cannot direct them to a 'model' establishment. They must also be able to choose which detainees they wish to interview and demand that such *meetings be confidential, without the presence of a member of the prison staff. If this confidentiality is not guaranteed, the ICRC, for instance, will refuse to visit prisons. Finally, some discreet investigations are made in those countries that refuse to follow the rules. Information is collected by prisoners' lawyers and families, without the administration knowing. This kind of investigation is undertaken by organisations such as Amnesty International, the FIDH or other human rights groups.*

The rich and the rest

Prison is a caricature of society insofar as it reproduces it, but in quite particular circumstances. Prison forms a community governed by power, domination and submission, but also by positive social relations. What brings the world of prison closest to the real world is the depth of its poverty, all the more unbearable by reason of its exceptions. A lot of prisons, in fact, contain a wing for white-collar criminals. The rich enjoy relatively favourable conditions, either because they pay for them or because of their high social standing. They are rarely sentenced to long terms and are generally in prison only for a short time. Prison thus reproduces society's class structures, with its modes of domination and its privileges and, as it is closed off from the outside world, these take on intolerable proportions when contrasted with the inhumane poverty of prison life.

The differences between these two worlds are manifold, the most notable being the fact that prisons are single-sex worlds, either all-male or all female.

Those Latin American prisons which house powerful drug traffickers have taken prison inequalities to extremes. The late Colombian drug baron, Pablo Escobar, ran his business from his prison cell just as he wanted. I have even seen wealthy prisoners invest in improving the prison where they were held, the better to carry out their activities and, quite incidentally, improve the common lot of the other detainees. Quite a few of them thus acquire the status of benefactor. In Yemen, a very rich young man imprisoned for killing his uncle over an inheritance had whole wings of the prison where he was held renovated. He also had small rooms built where the detainees could meet their families in private. He was treated with high regard and could go wherever he wished within the building. He was clearly adored by the prisoners. Rich prisoners usually have servants who are recruited among the poorer detainees. They buy their services to carry out the chores theoretically assigned to all prisoners. Here is another example of the replication in prison of the stratified economic relations prevailing in all societies.

Influential convicts in fact benefit from all sorts of exceptional treatment. In 1999 in Morocco, one scandal was the talk of the town: a well-known figure in society was supposed to have been serving a prison sentence when the police stopped him in his car one night for a traffic offence. In fact, he went in and out of prison at will. In the early 1970s, when the former Tunisian minister Ahmed Ben Salah was in prison, everybody knew that he went out regularly. Rich or well-known people thus have an easier time in detention than do the poor.

But these cases should not let us forget that prison is above all a hell on earth, a place where you cannot escape being locked up with prison guards and promiscuity. Such an environment only serves to multiply tenfold the hate prisoners feel for each other and sometimes for themselves. Moral misery, emotional deprivation and intellectual poverty are thus combined with physical squalor, while sexual deprivation is endured as one of the worst features. In Tunisian prisons, which I know well for having stayed in them a long time, those with the means and who have got into the authorities' good books have what they call their 'horse', that is, a young minion. There are sometimes fights and even killings among cell bosses for possession of these young inmates.

Fear, order and violence

Individual cells are very rare in prison. Where they do exist, they serve as punishment cells. Prison life is organised around large cells, which are usually overcrowded. In many developing countries, ever more prisoners sleep on the floor or in bunk beds. There are even prisons, in Moscow and in Jordan among other places, where prisoners have to sleep in shifts. As a result of the policy of over-reliance on prisons, the volume of space and air available to each prisoner has reduced considerably in recent years, prompting frequent crises, as well as problems of health and hygiene.

In most cases, a number of communal cells open onto a courtyard where prisoners are allowed out at set times. The minimum time outdoors required by international standards is one hour a day and, with a few exceptions, this minimum is respected. There are even prisons where the cell doors are open all day long. When the cell is jam-packed, this eases the everyday pressure, as it is the only way you can manage to bear the promiscuity. Otherwise, the occupants of each cell are allowed out in turn into the courtyard.

The authorities designate a cell chief, who is usually chosen for his physical strength and power to inspire fear. Very often he will have his own bodyguards and his enforcers, who make sure his orders are respected. He is a real gangster boss. This mode of organisation, as I've said, is encouraged by the prison administration. Prison management is, in fact, based on fear. The warders' uniform, their guns and their truncheons are also intended to create fear. Only in a few countries, such as Great Britain, are prison guards unarmed. Order must reign in prison: in the last resort, this is the only criterion for good prison management; the only thing that is really expected from a prisoner is submission. That's why all relations within prisons are based on the power relation between the dominant and the dominated. Guards have to demonstrate their power regularly, which explains their habit of beating and humiliating prisoners at the first sign of their stepping out of line.

Hierarchies of power are thus added to existing economic and social stratification, usually as deliberate systems set up with the connivance or outright instigation of the authorities. This system is based on fear, not respect; power-relations, not the rule of law; order, not rules. It relies on domination but also the management of needs. In many poor countries, the official daily expenditure per prisoner is no more than Euro 0.4 cents. There are prisons where the daily ration for prisoners is a bowl of rice or millet, distributed in wheelbarrows once a day. This was the situation I saw in Burkina Faso in 1997. In other prisons, lunch and dinner are supplied at the same time. Other countries try to supply three meals per day, however modest.

These are therefore contrasting situations, but in many countries, prisoners go hungry all the time and are prepared to do anything for extra rations. The better-off prisoners, on the other hand, receive food, clothing, cigarettes and money from their families, and get other prisoners to work for them by distributing a few crumbs of their wealth. Relations among prisoners are thus also regulated by each one's level of deprivation. We should remember that most prisoners come from poor backgrounds and that, after their first few months in prison, their families – who usually lack the means anyway– no longer provide for them. Their deprivations also explain how they can sell themselves physically to answer their most basic needs of survival. In prison, the feeling of dignity is dulled and people are prepared to sell their bodies and accept the unacceptable, abandoning their self-respect.

Punishment is an integral part of this system, even if techniques differ from one country to the next. It is part and parcel of the policy of maintaining order and bears no relation to the principle of rehabilitation that should guide all treatment to which prisoners are subjected.

The reason for this is that all prison life is based on violence. Two sorts of violence coexist and reinforce each other to compound the misery of prisoners. Violence among prisoners is sometimes harder to bear than that exercised by the prison authorities, because it is constant 24/7 violence, whereas the warders are not present all the time. It is integral to domination as part of prison life. The types of violence used by the cell leaders and bosses are many and varied. Beatings are the most common, but victims may also be obliged to sleep next to the toilets, in the hottest or coldest corners, and, as we have seen, sexual violence is also very common.

The authorities also clamp down on the prisoners, beating them, shaving the heads of the stubborn ones, sometimes stripping them naked. There are very few countries in which you can state with certainty that physical violence does not exist in prison. Prisoners can also be punished by denying them their rights, such as not allowing them visits, letters, parcels, or indeed any contact with the outside world. Another form of punishment is isolation, which, although in theory regulated, is in fact used illegally in a totally arbitrary fashion. Prisoners may be kept isolated for years on end. I myself was kept in total isolation for a year and a half. Frequently used against political prisoners, this punishment is also used on common-law prisoners considered – more often than not without any clear criteria – as violent and dangerous. For fear of danger determines most of the arbitrary measures taken by prison warders. I know of one case where, after a prisoner took advantage of his visitors to obtain drugs, the reaction of the authorities was to punish not only that individual, but all the prisoners collectively by placing bars and glass screens between them and their visitors. That is how all prisons become high security centres, even when they don't need to be.

Risky cohabitation

The first mistake lies in putting remandees – in theory innocent until proved guilty – together with convicted prisoners. The second is the scandalous mixing of juveniles with adults. In some countries, children under ten are put in the same cells as adults, despite international standards which give fourteen as the minimum age for imprisonment. Being more vulnerable and impressionable, with different needs from those of adults, juvenile offenders below the age of penal majority should in theory be placed in specialised centres.

Moreover, the international legal instruments on juvenile delinquency state that detention should be used only as a last resort. The best way to manage delinquency is to avoid detention for young people, as the worst scenario is for budding criminals to be left together. If detention is unavoidable, then the specialist centres where they are placed should serve as re-education units. Many countries – Tunisia, Palestine and Jordan among others – pretend to comply with international standards by calling their youth prisons 'rehabilitation centres', without actually changing anything but the name. Such countries put on an act and try to convince themselves that they are engaged in penal reform policies when they are not.

When young people are mixed in with adults, the worst can and does happen, because they are exploited by adults and have to serve them in all senses, including as sex objects. By the same token, young people may also learn to become criminals. Given their tender age, they are less able to resist the examples set by adults and learn quickly. Prison criminalises young offenders, sometimes beyond recall. Segregating them is therefore not only for their own protection, but also to protect society from the further spread of criminality.

The case of women is different because, apart from a few cases, they are usually segregated from men. More often than not, they are kept in the same prison, but in a separate wing, which can also lead to unacceptable situations. The rules that need respecting to avoid this are well known: the prison staff who have direct contact with women detainees should all be women, so as to avoid any risk of abuse from men. Where mixed prisons have wings reserved for women, the risk of such abuse is indeed greater than in all-female prisons.

The most extreme case I have seen is at Rilima prison in Rwanda. From August 1994, men, women and children were all mixed together there, with women's cells situated in the midst of the men's. You can just imagine what goes on there. I saw several women who had been in the prison for several years, with their babies. In another country, which I will refrain from naming, the female director of a women's prison was accused of conniving with a senior army officer to supply him with 'fresh flesh'. Elsewhere, in a capital city where the women's prison is situated inside a barracks, I was told that pretty young girls who refused to sleep with army officers were subjected to all kinds of ill-treatment. These are of course extreme cases, but ones that demonstrate the risks involved in mixing men and women prisoners together.

Furthermore, under-age girls are only rarely separated from adult women. Because there are few women convicts, it is difficult to maintain multiple places of detention. Yet, in women's prisons young girls run the same risks of learning criminal ways and being exploited, including sexually, as do youngsters in all-male prisons.

There are also many young children in prison, staying with their mothers. Without giving an exact age, the international standards allow nursing infants to stay with their mother until they are weaned, i.e. until they are eighteen months to two years old. Some countries, such as Lebanon, do not accept babies in prison. I know of one case of a woman imprisoned two weeks after giving birth. Her baby was brought to her twice a day to be breastfed, but not for more than five minutes at a time and she could not keep the baby with her. This regulation is inhumane, as it is harmful for both mother and child. On the other hand, some countries allow children to stay with their mothers until they are four to six years old. I even saw, in Nepal, a child of four living with his father in jail because he had no family outside the prison to take care of him. The presence of very small children naturally creates specific needs. In most cases, the state does not take care of them and it is usually NGOs or charities which step in to fill the gap.

The presence of voluntary associations in prison is common to every country in the world, including the richest. Nowhere, in fact, does the state take care of all prison needs, even when – as in rich countries – it may partly finance the work of specialised NGOs. Their presence is moreover very positive, as they create an additional link between the detainee and society, as well as those he or she may manage to maintain with their family.

Apart from women and young people, many other vulnerable categories of people live in prison, starting with those who are alcohol- or drug-dependent. The situation of drug users is generally much more precarious than for ordinary detainees. They are sometimes prepared to commit crimes in order to get hold of drugs. And so they may volunteer to act as henchmen for the cell bosses and, of course, to sell themselves physically to get their fix. They need special care in drug treatment centres, especially if they were convicted of an offence driven by their habit. Offenders who have committed theft to procure their drugs should be helped rather than punished. It is not easy and they often re-offend, but society should help them free themselves of their habit. Here, too, voluntary bodies are very active, alongside and instead of the state.

Lastly, political prisoners constitute a quite separate category within prison. In the space of a few years, their numbers have dwindled considerably around the world. But those that remain always experience the paradoxical situation that they are both feared and ill-treated. Although they are subject to various types of discrimination, they usually manage to obtain some of their demands because they enjoy international support and are often surrounded by an aura of celebrity. Unlike ordinary prisoners, their conditions of detention may evolve according to the political climate and the degree of exposure they enjoy internationally. Outside solidarity is rarely expressed for common-law prisoners. It is the politicals and more especially those branded 'prisoners of conscience' who benefit from it. Solidarity for them has now exceeded the scope of human rights organisations, as the UN has adopted a Convention for the Protection of Human Rights Defenders and set up mechanisms for their special protection.

A pathogenic environment

The many sick people in prison also constitute a category of vulnerable prisoners. There is usually at least one nurse in each prison, often a prisoner who worked as a nurse before his or her detention. Properly managed prisons include an infirmary stocked with medicines where detainees can be seen by a doctor, though in the poorest countries these provisions are missing. Not only do these prisons lack medical staff, they don't even have any medical supplies. As always, families with means to do so buy medication for their relatives, which raises the issue of equal access to health care. Theoretically, when the state deprives citizens of their freedom, its duty is to guarantee them basic health care. This is generally not the case, even though added vigilance is needed in prison, given that detention renders people more prone to illness because of overcrowding, promiscuity and lack of fresh air and exercise.

Prison is a pathogenic environment. This is especially true in poor countries where basic rules of hygiene are not respected: wastewater drains away where it can, latrines overflow and release noxious smells. This is not an exceptional state of affairs; it is unfortunately very common. The spread of contagious diseases is a major problem in prisons. Tuberculosis and AIDS are endemic in many countries and rife in prisons. In Russia and other former Soviet republics, tuberculosis affects tens of thousands of prisoners. PRI works in Russia and Kazakhstan to try to contain it, in association with a Dutch AIDS-prevention NGO. Other bodies such as Médecins sans Frontières, Médecins du Monde and the International Red Cross are very active in this field, as is the World Health Organization (WHO). The speed with which these diseases can spread in prison is frightening. In Uganda and elsewhere in Africa, whole wings are occupied solely by prisoners suffering from AIDS.

To try and reduce pathogenic factors in prison, PRI has carried out an interesting project to treat human waste in a Rwandan prison, where it helped set up a bio-gas and fertiliser production unit. This has been a success: the water is no longer polluted and the immediate environment around the prison has been cleaned up, with the added bonus of producing energy and fertiliser. This programme was funded by the United Kingdom and the

Netherlands, and PRI's assessment study shows that it deserves to be replicated.

The risk of contagion is not confined to prison. When prisoners are released back into society, they can easily contaminate other people around them, particularly because, as delinquents, their moral conscience may not be fully developed. With regard to AIDS, for example, they may make no effort to protect others. This is another reason why it is vital that health-care in prison should be treated as an integral part of public health services under the control of the responsible line ministries.

Prisoners and the outside world

Maintaining close contact between a prisoner and his home community should be the rule for all good management of detention and crime prevention. It is only on this condition that a prisoner can retain his humanity, by remaining responsible for others, especially his children, and keeping a sense of belonging to a community other than that imposed on him in prison. It also helps him not to lose hope. Convicted prisoners should accordingly be held as close to home as possible. This is the basis for any rehabilitation policy, because by staying in touch with the outside world, the prisoner cannot lose sight of the rules that regulate social life. Life in prison should in fact diverge as little as possible from normal life.

Unfortunately, this principle is more often than not forgotten by the prison authorities. At the least misdemeanour, they will ban all correspondence, stop all visits or cut the prisoner off from any information, even if such punishments are illegal by international standards. In stressing the coercive side of prison, the authorities tend to forget that time spent in prison should also be used to help detainees learn how to take charge of themselves again. Quite apart from being illegal, these punishments go against all logic, insofar as they serve to make prisoners more aggressive.

Here again, there are blatant inequalities, not only between countries, but also within the same country or the same prison. They should not be confused with the necessary differentiation in treatment between different categories of prisoners. Those at the end of their sentences can in some cases go outside the prison, among other things to look for work, with the help of social workers. Unfortunately, in the developing countries in the South, different treatments are more often the result of corruption than of a good rehabilitation policy. Because of the prison management's habitual obsession with security, prisoners are often physically separated from their visitors and are not allowed to touch them. In other countries, though, such as Morocco, Yemen, France and Italy, conjugal visits are allowed for a few hours or for a whole weekend. This right to sexual intimacy is all the more precious in that it helps reduce sexual violence considerably, as well as violence in general in prison.

Another way of maintaining links to the outside world is to provide recreational activities for the detainees. In this regard, things have improved considerably over the last few years, with efforts to open prisons up to leisure activities. In many countries, prisoners can take part in cultural activities, in drama groups, music, drawing, painting, ceramics and craft-work. This is no longer an exceptional situation and it is, fortunately, spreading to countries in the South. Thus, in Senegal, prisoners who can paint are able to hold annual exhibitions, and there is now an annual fair for arts and crafts produced in prison. Tunisia also organises an annual exhibition of artwork produced by prisoners. In Palestine, education is very much encouraged in prisons, with some detainees catching up with their school studies and passing their exams with flying colours. Other countries, unfortunately, try to prevent political prisoners from pursuing any studies and generally only relent after tireless campaigns by the prisoners themselves.

Where authorities don't actively support such opportunities, they usually allow them to happen. Sport is also encouraged as an important part of the physical and mental health of detainees. It can even serve to counteract the depressive and morbid tendencies in many prisoners. Vocational training has also developed, as many countries have realised that by supporting professional training, they will be promoting the social rehabilitation of prisoners. Actually, any means are good that will stop prisoners being idle, which is harmful to their physical and mental equilibrium and leaves them more open to the contagion of criminality.

To balance this picture, however, it should be noted that this sort of activity is only available to a tiny minority of detainees world-wide. For example, only 3,000–4,000 out of the 125,000 prisoners in Rwanda are occupied in this way. In Jordan, this kind of occupation only concerns 10 per cent of the prison population of around 7,000. This approach is thus developing, but remains very limited, as are its prospects of expanding, for material and financial reasons among others.

Work in prison

Forced labour for prisoners is now illegal under international standards. In many cases, however, they cannot refuse to work, but are paid to do so. Remandees are not obliged to work but can do so if they wish. In fact, the issue is not whether they want to work, but if they are able to do so, as it depends upon the prison being able to provide work for them. Only a derisory number of detainees are able to work, in reality. Should this possibility be increased? This is a difficult and controversial question, insofar as, while work can be a tool for social reintegration, prisoners are also all too often considered as a cheap labour force to be exploited.

Work may be carried out for the prison management or for an outside body. Prisoners may thus be employed in the construction or repair of public buildings. They may work in hospitals or schools or be assigned to street cleaning. The administration may also 'lend' them to private companies. This can take the form of a contract with a businessman setting up a workshop inside prison, providing the raw materials and collecting the finished product against payment of an agreed amount. Usually, the administration gives back part to the prisoners in some form or other. The International Labour Organisation (ILO) has regulated prisoners' pay, so as to prevent exploitation. Prisoners' pay should, in theory, be fair. Other companies may require work done in their own facilities and then will take responsibility for transporting the prisoners to the place of work and back. Part of the prison population may thus be integrated into the system of production.

The most frequent conflicts occur over pay, whether the prisoners work for the public or the private sector. In many cases, in effect, they don't receive any money and are paid in kind. They may receive extra meals or manufactured goods that they make themselves, when these are consumer products such as clothes. It sometimes happens that work itself is seen as a privilege, where detainees are often happy to leave their overcrowded cells for a few hours per day. Some may even pay the foremen to be hired on work teams. In prison, work is a much coveted commodity. When prisoners receive a salary, it is often notional and does not correspond to prevailing social standards. In Jordan, they are paid around 50 cents (U.S.) per day. In most countries, prisoners can earn ten to fifteen U.S. dollars a month. Prison work is therefore profitable both for the prison managers and the public authorities.

The ILO tries to remedy these injustices by declaring illegal products made in the prisons of certain countries where the situation is particularly scandalous, such as in China. This country has, in practice, kept on a tradition of totalitarian states where, from Stalinist Russia to Nazi Germany, forced labour by prisoners was a vital element in the chain of production. Forced labour by prisoners is a modern form of that kind of slavery so often employed in antiquity for large infrastructural building works. Having said this, it is not clear whether boycotting products produced in prison is effective; but it can be used as a tactic by human rights defenders who believe it to be of great importance and regard it as a matter of principle.

One of the commonest types of prison work is the use of prisoners by prison staff for their private needs. It is common practice for prison directors or their colleagues to have their own houses built by free prison labour. In many developing countries, prison guards have prisoners cultivating their piece of land. In Uganda, the land surrounding a prison near Kampala is cultivated by prisoners for the benefit of the warders. In this case, too, the prisoners consider themselves privileged: they can go outside, have contact with the warders' families, and sometimes earn a bit of money for their work.

In this sector as in others, prisoners try above all to escape, at least for some of the time, from a situation they find intolerable.

6

DO PRISONERS HAVE RIGHTS?

Everywhere in the world, perception of and respect for prisoners' rights are evolving far too slowly, in spite of their ever more precise definition by international standards being more or less accepted by the majority of states. It is still difficult, even today, to conceive of offenders and criminals as having rights. It is, however, by the degree of respect for these rights that the level of civilisation of a society can be measured. And by this yardstick, the most civilised countries are not necessarily those you might think.

There are the worst, those where a totalitarian system has managed to make the prison system utterly opaque. These regimes – from North Korea to Cuba, Syria, Saudi Arabia or China – cultivate secrecy; they prefer two types of detention: clandestine prisons that do not officially exist and the system of concentration camps, as in China. These are where prisoners' living conditions are often closer to hell than to humanity. As you might expect, it is not easy to obtain information about what happens inside them and even less so to intervene.

There are also countries where the law is flouted, not so much from any deliberate political intent, but owing to an exceptional situation. This is the case today in Rwanda, a strange 'land of a thousand prisons', which it is worth pausing here to consider.

The slow process of developing laws

The aim of imprisonment is, of course, above all to protect society; but it is also the duty of legislators and administrators to guarantee the rights of everyone, including those who have broken the law and ended up in prison. The primary right is that of preserving someone's physical and moral integrity, that's to say, the right not to be tortured, humiliated or raped, and it is non-negotiable. Under international law, the only right prisoners are deprived of is freedom to move around. In theory, therefore, they may enjoy all the other rights. They should live in decent conditions that maintain their dignity; they must be fed, clothed and housed normally. They also have a right to health, information, education and work, wherever possible.

The international instruments regulating prisoners' rights, some of which are non-derogable, ought to be translated into national laws and put into practice. The problem is that no society will accept that conditions in prison should be better than living conditions among the poorest classes. Wherever you go, you will find that public opinion does not accept the need to respect prisoners' rights. Nowhere are they considered self-evident, even among the better-educated classes.

Most often, public opinion cannot understand that prisoners' rights are not privileges. In countries where they are nonetheless granted, this public indifference allows the authorities to chip away at them, which they usually do without fail. Improvements are never deemed irreversible, and never secured once and for all. A change of government, or even a simple change of prison commissioner, can put them at risk. Improving prison conditions thus remains a topical issue, especially now that it is obligatory under international law.

The ethical basis of this law, as we have seen, was set by the UN Charter and Universal Declaration of Human Rights, which established the principles of respect for human dignity. To these fundamental texts were added the four Geneva Conventions of 1954, defining humanitarian law. This preliminary work opened the way for a definition of standards of detention, i.e. the basis on which a state should have the right to deprive someone of their liberty. As with all other rights, this in return implies certain obligations, such as to ensure that detention takes place within a framework of respect for human rights, starting with the physical and moral integrity of the individual.

The most detailed normative text on this subject is, as we have seen, the United Nations Standard Minimum Rules for the Treatment of Prisoners (1955). Over the years, other texts have come to complement this one. The UN International Covenant on Civil and Political Rights, promulgated in 1966, represented an important step forward in international law. Then, during the 1970s and 1980s, the United Nations finalised international standards for the detention of juveniles and developed codes of ethics for the judiciary – magistrates, judges and lawyers. The development of international law reached a landmark in 1990 with the adoption of a fundamental text by the UN General Assembly, urging member states to apply non-custodial sentencing.[1] Most of these texts do not have the weight of a convention and are therefore not legally binding, but they have acquired an important normative value by reason of being adopted by consensus in the General Assembly, and states the world over recognise this value. The legal basis of prison law therefore exists and does not need to be reinvented.[2]

This evolution is still continuing today, through the development of a corpus of international law on certain modern types of crime, such as organised transnational crime (the most advanced project), human trafficking, drug trafficking and terrorism, as well as Internet crime. All of this work involves reflection on the meaning of detention and sentencing, and on the need for a system to protect society, taking full account of respect for the individual.

Good and bad learners

No country in the world can escape criticism of the way it treats its prisoners. Even those that respect human rights the most have been caught out at one time or another. The European Committee

1. The UN *Standard Minimum Rules for Non-Custodial Sanctions (The Tokyo Rules)*, 1990.
2. See PRI's 1995 handbook, *Making Standards Work*, which describes and analyses the UN standards for sentencing and detention and explains the rules that international law-makers sought to institute. Revised 2001.

for the Abolition of Torture and Inhuman or Degrading Treatment, which, along with the European Court of Human Rights, is the implementing body for the European Human Rights Charter, has targeted more than one EU member-state in recent years, including even the Scandinavians, reputedly the most compliant with penal law. Others, including France, have been condemned by the European Court for acts of torture. In these democratic countries, it is usually people from minority groups who bear the brunt of degrading treatment.

Bearing in mind these reservations, it should be said that the states with long-standing democratic traditions are obviously those with the least disrespect for prisoners' rights, and that the Scandinavian states unquestionably come first in terms of their respect for the individual. In Denmark, the prison guards' union has long imposed a ban on overcrowding in detention centres and on building new ones. From the 1990s, a waiting list was accordingly drawn up for convicted offenders, who served their sentences only once places in prison fell vacant. Since then, however, the country has built new prisons, and has thus returned to the norm.

Apart from overcrowding, an important criterion for prisoners' treatment is the ratio of people of all categories working in places of detention to the number of prisoners held. In the early 1980s, the Netherlands had the highest ratio in the world, with one and a half employees per prisoner. This was not a luxury, contrary to what most people believe, but proof of good management. Here again, the best ratios are found in northern Europe. The significant steps forward in these countries in recent years have helped legitimise the standards set by the UN, by showing they can be achieved. In the field of penal reform, as in other areas, we hear more and more about 'good practice' – and rightly so, since it should not remain an exception, but serve as an example for replication.

These good examples can be found everywhere, even if they are still somewhat limited in number. In France, there are a few model prisons, one of which (in Bastia, Corsica) has detainees freely going to work outside. In Andra Pradesh, India, an open prison has been in operation for over fifty years for those serving life imprisonment. It is a kind of village ringed by barriers, where convicts who have already spent many years in jail can live openly. They are transferred there on condition that their family agrees to live with them, and they are entirely self-supporting, going to work outside the village and living as part of a family. To benefit from this status, they have to agree to respect certain rules, such as never spending a night outside the village. Other detainees may, after serving part of their sentence, be confined to their own homes. The invention of electronic tagging, which makes it possible to keep prisoners under surveillance, has led to a more widespread application of these measures. I have already mentioned prison farms, such as the ones in Zambia. Elsewhere, NGOs may find different ways of working with prisoners. In Lebanon, for instance, one group organises open-air holiday/work camps for young offenders.

Such good examples are thus not limited to the older democratic nations; many countries in the South are also putting them into practice. Besides, they don't only involve petty offenders but may also work for hardened criminals. What all these experiments have in common is their aim to rehabilitate prisoners rather than being intended for society to exact revenge. Within the same country they can coexist with traditional prisons where detainees are treated much more harshly. But, for these new types of prison to exist, there has to be a real political will to humanise the system. Within this overall framework, the character of those in charge of prisons can also influence policy in the direction either of greater humanisation or of toughening up.

This is why, as long as basic rules of comfort are respected, it is not necessarily the most modern prisons that are the most humane. The town of Ngosi, in Burundi, has two prisons for men and one for women. One of them was built according to the state of the art. Yet this is the one with the most serious overcrowding and neglect of prisoners. In 1996, an epidemic broke out there, causing some 300 casualties. In the older, more run-down men's prison, detainees are able to cook their own food and spend most of their days in the communal yard.

Conversely, although it is virtually impossible to get any information about them, countries with the harshest prison conditions are those under the most brutal dictatorships, such as Iraq or North Korea. Among democratic countries, the United States is an exception in its treatment of prisoners. First of all, as we've already said, the prison population is drawn mostly from ethnic and racial minorities. African-Americans, who represent only 12 per cent of the country's population, nevertheless account for over half the prison population. It is estimated that six or seven out of every ten young black men have at one time or another had a brush with the law.

Nor is the United States a role model for human rights observance: it has ratified hardly any of the international conventions designed to protect them. Few outside critics seem able to influence the country's behaviour. In the human rights NGOs, we often wonder if we should try to shame U.S.A. for retaining the death penalty, for its retreat into zero tolerance, or for the conditions which hold sway in its prisons. We feel as if we are hitting our heads against a wall. America's unshakeable conviction that she is always in the right has something inhuman about it.

Other democratic countries, like Japan, can be criticised just as much for the way they treat their prisoners. The harsh prison conditions in Japan, such as the ban on prisoners talking to or looking at the guards, may in part be put down to cultural and social differences. History testifies to the brutality of Japanese behaviour in the countries they conquered and occupied in the first half of the twentieth century. To this day, marginal groups outside the mainstream are systematically discriminated against.

The ghost gulag

The worst situations outside all rule of law are in those secret prisons whose existence we don't know about, whose occupants are left to die in silence, far from the world's view. In the late 1980s, word got out about these ghost prisons, whose existence was rumoured and denounced, from Morocco to Sudan, North Korea to China. From that time on, testimony started to pour in, even though it is difficult to get reliable statistics on such places, which are by definition secret. This doesn't prevent the vital work of researching and exposing them, even if we know it will remain incomplete, since such regimes are past masters at hiding their misdeeds.

The unique case of Rwanda

Tens of thousands of prisoners charged with taking part in the 1994 genocide are rotting in Rwandan jails. The case of Rwanda is unique given the nature of the accusation, the ratio of detainees to the country's population (the highest in the world), the limited capacity of the prison system, and the near-total destruction of the administration of justice after the genocide and the ensuing war. There were still 130,000 prisoners four years after the genocide. Some had been released, but only a few, while others were still being arrested. By 2002, the prison situation in Rwanda was still virtually the same as it had been at the end of 1994, and this looks set to go on for a long time.

Hoping to break this log jam, the then director of prisons was sent to represent Rwanda at the Pan-African Conference on Prison Conditions in Africa, organised by PRI in Kampala in September 1996. PRI's first direct contact with the Rwandan government, however, did not take place until April 1997, when the European Commission asked it to send an assessment mission to Rwanda to look into the possibility of providing support for the prison service in managing penal custody in that country. This mission allowed PRI to ascertain that there was real political will on the part of the Rwandan government, which prompted our decision to get involved, especially as the European Union, soon joined by the British, Dutch, Swiss and Swedes, gave PRI the means to do so.

The mission revealed a strange situation. Rwanda had nineteen official detention centres, as well as a multitude of informal lock-ups (known as *cachots*). These nineteen centres, spread across the country, work like central prisons. Staffed by former soldiers, and supervised by Military Security, they were out of bounds to the prison authorities, at least for the first few years. The other lock-ups, set up in makeshift quarters during the crisis, are totally lacking in proper infrastructure. Starting off as temporary accommodation, over the years they had turned into permanent detention centres. Each of them held several thousand people – half the total prison population – and they had become dumps, creating a real catastrophe for their surroundings. Tons of human waste lay exposed to the elements, and a noxious odour fouled the air for miles around. The prison staff, most of them former soldiers, hadn't a clue what their duties were and proved to be totally incompetent.

None of these prisons had qualified staff, and those that had were nothing like enough: only 300 prison guards were assigned to oversee more than 100,000 detainees! Nsinda prison alone, with some 12,000 inmates, is supervised and managed by only forty people all told, from the director down to the orderlies. To make their daily fare more bearable, the prisoners themselves took the initiative to grow crops in fields around the prison up to forty kilometres away, and sold their produce at local markets. With their earnings, they bought a truck. The prison was really run by self-management and, in spite of the lack of prison guards, very few prisoners escaped. Most of the detainees were therefore people who didn't really need to be locked up at all. As for the prison administration, it was down to a bare minimum: its female director had three assistants in all. The prison has subsisted since then on dramatically reduced means. When I was there, it provided no food at all to the prisoners.

The official prisons were entirely taken care of by the International Red Cross. In 2001, the ICRC still supplied half the food for the nineteen central prisons, the other prisoners being fed entirely by their families. The ICRC had at the time, in fact, refused to feed them so as not to encourage their continued confinement in these premises.

The situation has improved slightly since my first mission in 1997, but it is still far from being settled. Things have started to move, though, despite the transfer of responsibility for prisons from the Department of Justice to the Ministry of the Interior in 1999. The justice system has started to be rebuilt with international aid, as has the legal profession. In 1995, just twenty-five lawyers were left in Rwanda, only one of them a Hutu. It was Avocats sans Frontières (Lawyers beyond Borders) that took on some of the defence of both accused and victims. Today there are more than sixty practising lawyers in Rwanda.

For the time being, only 2,500 remand prisoners have gone on trial, a mere drop in the ocean! This slow processing is the most serious problem facing Rwandan justice. While they await trial, hundreds of detainees die in prison each year as a result of their deplorable living conditions, marked by hunger and contagious disease. According to official sources, Rwandan prisons register a horrendous death-toll every year. Yet there is little hope of seeing a significant drop in the number of prisoners in the short term.

The situation is even more worrying in that, since 1994, Rwanda has not built a single new prison. Only one has been rebuilt and others have been renovated thanks to international aid, in particular a women's prison that had been in a particularly parlous state. The construction of a large prison complex intended to accommodate those who have been tried and sentenced to long prison terms is now under way, with Dutch funding.

From January 1998, PRI started to intervene practically to improve the prison situation. First, we systematically trained prison staff, from the warders to the officers in charge. Our fundraising efforts enabled the prison management to recruit new specialised staff, which we had trained. Thus each prison was provided with clerks and accountants.

We then fostered the growth of productive activities inside the prisons. In several of them, this had started before our arrival, at the prisoners' own initiative, hoping to use their skills to improve their meagre fare. This was how, as we've seen, some agricultural engineers began to cultivate fields and raise livestock around their places of detention. Elsewhere, fish farming was preferred, where there were ponds. We also helped develop crafts in prison by installing carpentry, clothing and motor-repair workshops, as well as vocational training for prisoners in these trades.

Our first aim was thus to make the prison management and personnel more professional and to promote the development of prison industries. Our work is now entering a second phase during which our support for small-scale production will be reduced so as to invest in larger projects.

In 2000, the Government of Rwanda called on us to create alternatives to imprisonment. It realised that, if things were left to go on at the present rate, bringing all the remand prisoners to trial could take several decades. It has therefore set up traditional local courts, known as *gacaca*, which can speed up the process and hand down non-custodial sentences as an alternative to imprisonment. A law to this effect was passed and applied by decrees promulgated in August 2001. It stipulates that those who confess their crimes will benefit from mitigating circumstances and half their prison sentence will have to be commuted to community service. For the first time in history, those accused of crimes against humanity will simply be given an alternative sentence. PRI helped bring this law into being by hosting an expert seminar in

Rwanda and by helping draft the decree applying community
service.

The nature of our involvement in Rwanda has thus changed
according to the evolving needs of the situation and the
requirements of the authorities. We must hope that, by using the
modern form of traditional justice that is *gacaca*, it will be possible
to close down the makeshift prisons, freeing those remandees
whose guilt has not been clearly established and transferring those
convicted to regular prisons.

Implementing *gacaca*

The new Rwandan law requires that traditional justice should be
administered by courts made up of lay judges, elected by the
community but assisted by trained court officials. These courts
will sit at all levels of the provincial administration, from the
village to the *préfecture* (provincial headquarters). The law
foresees the creation of 11,000 such courts, each comprising
nineteen judges. They will hear defendants and witnesses at public
sessions, the purpose of which is also intended to be cathartic. This
requires that the court proceedings be public and transparent, so
as to allow the population to accept the sentences. (This is a
country where, after all, the regime is still based on a demographic
minority.) Some 165,000 judges have thus been elected. Although
it may seem incongruous, since it is greater than the overall
number of prisoners, the large number of judges is itself considered
one of the factors conducive to national reconciliation.

We still don't know how this enormous and costly procedure
will function in practice. But no government in Rwanda could
allow the '*génocidaires*' to be released without having put them on
trial, at least symbolically. Part of the population would never
accept it and there would certainly be bloody acts of revenge
against the accused when they left prison. A regime led by the Tutsi
minority – representing only 14 per cent of the population –
cannot permit the instability that such behaviour might provoke,
especially as internal and border security are far from being
completely restored. The re-establishment of a minimum rule of
law is therefore essential, even if the cost is high.

On the basis of current assessments, it is thought that, with
these new tribunals, all those on remand may be brought to trial

within three to five years. In this context, PRI continues to support the prison administration in three main areas: continued financial support for the recruitment of specialised staff, setting up a system of in-house training by teams of trainers, and help with establishing a set of prison regulations for the treatment of prisoners.

At the same time, we have a team of researchers, including an ethnologist, following the *gacaca* courts and studying them as they are set up and beginning to operate. These researchers are tasked with reporting any problems encountered by the courts, including any negative aspects or mistakes, and alerting the line ministries and the international community to these. Rwanda needs our help in all these areas of work, especially as PRI, together with the ICRC, is the only international organisation providing hands-on assistance in prison reform. It is no coincidence that PRI's Kigali office is our biggest one, counting up to nineteen members of staff, seventeen of them Rwandans. This demonstrates the importance we attach to this country.

We should be aware, though, that for many years to come, Rwanda will still have the highest ratio of prisoners per head of population in the world, in spite of the government's obvious concern to get back to normal as soon as possible and the international pressure to do so. Instead of dropping, the prison population risks increasing at first, as the confessions made before the tribunals may generate new arrests. This risk is so real that many have been trying to flee since the grassroots system of justice was decided on, afraid of being denounced, whether rightly or not. We have, indeed, to take into account the risk of villagers settling their own scores, and some will jump at the chance to do so. Those who are lucky enough to be released will, moreover, demand the return of assets which in most cases were confiscated during their stay in prison, usually by Tutsis returning from exile abroad. During the time this justice system is being set up, we unfortunately have to expect all manner of abuses.

Many people wonder why the Rwandan authorities did not opt for the South African model of a Truth and Reconciliation Commission, such as was set up at the end of apartheid. The reason is that the two situations are entirely different. In spite of these differences, the Rwandan government has sought inspiration from South African solutions. Seminars have been held, as a result of which the government has set up three institutions it will work with: a National Human Rights Commission; the sixth chamber of the Supreme Court, responsible for the new *gacaca* tribunals; and a National Reconciliation Commission. There is also a Compensation Commission to provide reparations to the families of victims, at least in part, but it has not worked properly so far for lack of resources. Donors have proved unwilling to co-operate, accusing this commission of corruption and incompetence, while the government reproaches donors for not wanting to contribute financially to resolving the problems arising in the aftermath of genocide.

But we shouldn't give up hope. After all, it was not certain that PRI would manage to work in this country over the long term. Many had warned us of the obstacles in our path. We have nonetheless done it. PRI, as I have already said, can only be effective under certain conditions, including political will on the part of governments who seek our help, and the existence of people inside the country who can eventually take over our work. To date, these conditions have been met in Rwanda, despite the immense difficulties the country is going through, not least the insecurity. This relative success, in a context of mutual respect, sometimes surprises me. It's true that we have taken maximum precautions in every area. For its work in Rwanda, PRI surrounded itself with a small group of consultants who were well aware of all the problems. Our main concern, in fact, is not to get involved in internal squabbles and to remain true to an ethic drawn exclusively from human rights principles.

The global situation with regard to respect for prisoners' rights is thus full of contrasts. But gradually, often imperceptibly, the law moves forward. We must try to speed it up.

7

ALTERNATIVES TO PRISON

In every corner of the globe, there is no disputing the fact that prisons are too full, or that they are too often a school for crime and a means of excluding offenders, not a way of preparing them for their return to society after paying off their debt to it. Throughout the world, re-offending is too common not to present a dilemma for the whole institution of imprisonment.

In the U.S.A., the National Bureau of Statistics has calculated that 16 per cent of offenders released between 1986 and 1994, on completion of their first sentence, were back behind bars within three months. More in-depth research in Florida shows that the highest rates of re-offending are to be found among young people and blacks, that the rate of recidivism is inversely proportional to their educational levels, and that thieves re-offend more often than drug addicts. These studies also found that the prisoners serving their sentence in high security units are more likely to re-offend than all others. In New Zealand, 30 per cent of men and 17 per cent of women released in 1998–99 returned to prison during the course of the next year. In Canada, the re-offending rate reached 37 per cent at the end of one year and 65 per cent at the end of two. In Denmark, too, it reached 45 per cent after two years.[1] Although it is more difficult to establish such statistics for

---

1. International Centre for Prison Studies, *Analysis of International Policy and Practice in Reducing Re-offending by Ex-Prisoners*, London, Kings College, 2001.

*developing countries, the figures available show that recidivism is
far from being a peripheral problem.*

*For all these reasons, more and more experts now believe that
the need is urgent to create many more alternatives to prison, from
crime prevention and diversion to alternative sentencing and
rehabilitation in preparation for a return to ordinary life. In fact,
it is the whole point of imprisonment that has to be revised: what
types of punishment are effective, and for what offences? And
would it not be better to tackle the roots of crime rather than
punish offenders, by diverting marginal groups away from
delinquency that unfortunately is often socially conditioned?*

*Experiments are now being carried out in many places to
reduce the role of incarceration within the system of sanctions.
While they have yet to lead to significant policy changes, they do
offer new perspectives which may yet make it possible to break the
vicious circle of excessive use of custodial sanctions.*

Prevention is better

How do you prevent crime? Sociologists, political pundits and
criminologists will no doubt agree that the best prevention lies in
building a society whose members have access to education,
health-care and full employment, allowing them to fulfil their
essential needs, both material and spiritual. For it is frustration
that most often leads to crime. Bad examples should be avoided:
we know how harmful the influence of television can be in
glorifying violence and brute force. Today's heroes are often brutal
characters. The prevalence of violence in the media is bound to
encourage its development.

Prevention also means adopting measures on behalf of persons
and groups at risk, and minorities that have difficulty in adapting.
Crimes are often committed by those who feel excluded from
society and believe themselves to be thereby exempted from its
norms and duties. These marginal people do not recognise the
existence of limits not to be overstepped. They do not have the
same notions of good and bad conduct as the rest of society. For
people who are not granted their rights by society feel no sense of
obligation towards it. Hence the need to pay special attention to
those social categories and precarious situations that foster
criminality.

To make it easier for minorities to integrate, community policing may be the answer. Its role is not to repress, but to protect, give advice and offer help. Some experiments with community policing have produced positive results. Malawi has set up border surveillance to prevent trafficking in small arms with help from border communities, who are working with the police to combat this trade. Community policing is also clearly useful for monitoring breaches of traffic regulations: it can be a powerful tool for preventing driving offences. The ideal situation is one of complicity between the law-enforcement agents and the local population, but for this to happen, the police must act as helpers, not as adversaries.

It is also necessary to take care of certain categories of young people, to help them out of situations in which they are made to feel under-valued. Thus, several boroughs in the Greater London area provide literacy courses for linguistic minorities, to help them master English. So there are some intelligent policies for dealing with young people who are disoriented, lacking adult guidance and short of recreational facilities. Social workers can organise a range of activities for them and with them, to restore their self-esteem.

Those who underestimate this kind of response to delinquency, claiming that such measures alone cannot solve the problem, need reminding that criminality is marginal in all societies, and that taking action on the margins thus makes sense. Moreover, no study has yet shown that this kind of action does not have some impact, even if it is not always as effective as expected. Perhaps expectations are too high to start with. But experience shows that these activities, even if they remain small-scale, always bring some good to individuals, whether in a group, a building or a neighbourhood. There is always something to be gained by them. You would have to admit that the cost of these programmes is never too high when you consider that their human value is incalculable. The prevention of crime is obtained at this price. What is important is the protection of people's dignity by all means possible.

In fact, the term 'prevention' includes many kinds of activity and its nature differs greatly from one context to another. In societies that are still partly traditional, where neighbourly relations and family ties are strong, prevention occurs almost naturally, as part of the running of daily life. People know and observe each other. The problem is different in developed societies where individualistic behaviour is very much to the fore. The process of individualisation has led to a slackening of social control. An individual who is independent of the group acts in a way that is much more detached from his environment. This observation does not mean singing the praises of traditional societies: it is a statement of fact. In such societies, the collective conscience is very strong and its control over individuals very strict. When someone has no ties, he feels he has fewer obligations and his internalised self-control becomes weaker.

But the type of society in which we live isn't the only factor influencing our behaviour. Levels of education and affluence are equally important determinants. This is why, in modern societies, there needs to be a greater effort at prevention, with pro-active planning for it. Although it has a higher economic cost, its benefits in the long run are incalculable. It should also serve to recreate social bonds in order to reinstate protective safeguards.

We need to be aware that prevention is a long-term project that rarely produces immediate results. We have to be patient and be prepared to work over the long haul. Happily, this is being done here and there. In France, local authorities have implemented urban renewal programmes aimed at improving the daily life of those living in problem neighbourhoods, so as to pre-empt any risk of social and urban exclusion. At the level of prevention, this programme aims to strengthen the capacity of those individuals in contact with juveniles to spot their problems, and then involve professionals who have the skills to deal with them. There is a real network of educational support and preventive supervision that has been set up without actually creating any new structures. This programme also favours new methods for resolving conflicts before any judicial intervention occurs. An important component is the mobilisation of the whole community to help young people in difficulty as well as their families, so as to back up the implementation of any judicial rulings. In the same line of approach, several town councils and préfectures have set up multi-disciplinary teams of psychologists, drug prevention specialists and other social workers, targeting different categories of people at risk. In Saint-Denis, in the Parisian suburbs, one such team has for several years been caring for, counselling, following up, helping and listening to such people and this work is beginning to show results.

PRI is often actively involved in this preventive work with vulnerable groups. In Addis Ababa, we helped a local community-based organisation (CBO) to set up a programme to prevent juvenile delinquency in four slum areas with a total of 30,000 inhabitants. In the beginning, it concentrated mainly on clean-up operations, women's income-generating activities, funding schools and promoting community organising. We helped it build a programme directed at juvenile re-offenders by identifying twenty known delinquents under eighteen (sixteen boys and four girls), with the help of local community leaders. None of them had committed a serious offence or crime, but all these street children had been hardened by their repeated stays in prison. With our support, the CBO took care of these twenty youngsters for two years, providing psychological help and teaching each of them a trade. During this time and since, not one of these young people had any brush with the police. After two years, they were replaced by another group which received the same treatment. This pilot project had a 100 per cent success rate. At the 10th UN Congress for the Prevention of Crime in 2000 it was put forward as an example of good practice for crime prevention.

Two women's groups in Kampala, Uganda, have since 1994 been involved with rehabilitating women prisoners, with the backing of PRI. In Africa, women are generally imprisoned as a result of family conflicts over issues of inheritance, quarrels between co-wives or gender violence, and, once in detention, they lose all contact with their families, who abandon them. In most cases, their husbands desert them, and their children grow up without them and no longer need them. These women are extremely vulnerable, and as such are obvious candidates for the vicious cycle of criminality. The two Ugandan associations decided to take care of those who agreed to it during the latter part of their detention and for six months after their release. They built sheltered accommodation on a piece of land provided by the local authorities, classrooms for literacy classes and workshops for vocational training. After six months, the ex-prisoners left this centre, having been helped to find a job. Better still, realising they needed a small amount of capital to return to active life, these women set up their own association, again with help from the two NGOs, so as to have access to micro-credit. By 2000, out of three or four groups of women under their care since the beginning of the project, there had been only one case of re-offending. Here again is a long-term project that has produced good results.

What should replace prison?

In 1995–96, an important study was published by a French magistrate working in Senegal on alternatives to imprisonment in developing countries. After it appeared in the journal of the French Magistrates Union,[2] it was presented at a 1997 conference on Community Service in Africa organised by PRI in Zimbabwe. That shows how long we have been involved in this issue.

Alternatives to prison include the whole range of non-custodial sanctions and, beyond that, all the types of arrangements and compensations that arise between parties in dispute. These range from a simple verbal warning to financial or material compensation to halt the dispute before it is brought to justice, which may end up with one or other of the protagonists in prison. The person at fault can also be made to repair or replace a damaged asset. A judge may likewise rule that reparation can be made through unpaid work for the benefit of the community, hence the term 'community service'.[3]

The most commonly used non-custodial sanction world-wide is a suspended sentence. Fines also exist in most legal systems, but they have only limited impact given that those convicted often do not have the means to pay them and are therefore constrained in prison instead. Less frequently applied in developing countries is the alternative of conditional release (parole) with supervised conduct (probation), while developed countries, which have the necessary personnel – penal oversight judges or probation panels – employ this practice extensively. For those remanded in custody, bail may be an alternative. Bail is either financial, which applies only to those who can pay it, or moral, with a third party standing surety for the accused to ensure his appearance before the police or the court. This practice is rare in developing countries, but is used in Kenya and Zimbabwe.

2. Odette-Luce Bouvier, 'Alternatives to Incarceration in Developing Countries' *Justice* 153–55, July 1997–February 1998.
3. *Travaux d'intérêt public* or *Travaux d'intérêt général* in French.

Other alternatives have arisen in recent years from the need to ease congestion in prison. Electronic tagging is one of them: it makes it possible to check on the movements of a convicted person on parole or under house arrest; but for PRI it does not represent a miracle cure for prison, as is often claimed. For the time being, it can only be tried out in developed countries, given its fairly sophisticated technology that requires computerised electronic surveillance. Yet prison overcrowding is a critical issue the world over, not just for rich countries where, in any case, the use of electronic tagging is for the time being still limited. It is becoming more commonplace in the United States, where its use is nowadays most widespread. It was recently introduced into France, the United Kingdom and the Netherlands. Scandinavian countries still have reservations about its use, which may be seen as dehumanising, owing to the constant surveillance of those wearing tags and the intrusion this implies into their private life and that of their families.

Community service

Community service, nowadays growing rapidly as an alternative to prison, is often based on a tradition that pre-dates the coming of prisons. It was often a matter of simply picking up the idea again in many countries and familiarising the authorities and public opinion with it. In nearly all developed countries, it is now firmly in place among the range of sanctions available. In England and Wales it has been there for a long time. France, taking its cue from the English example, introduced it in the middle of the 1980s. The Scandinavian countries, the Netherlands, Belgium, the United States, Canada, and Australia have all made it a central element of their non-custodial sanctions, with widely differing results. The judicial ruling itself is everywhere identical: an offence legally punishable by prison is redeemed by a number of hours of unpaid work for the community (not for the victim or his family).

This type of punishment – and this is what makes it so original – requires the consent of the convicted person who may, if he prefers, choose to go to prison instead. It is also a modifiable penalty: it is adapted not only to the offender's skills but also to the time at his disposal. If he has a job, everything is done to help him keep it. He thus pays his debt to society outside his work

hours. To this end, he is monitored not only by the institution that
benefits from his work, but also by another person, either a paid
or voluntary social worker, or a probation officer. In France, it is
the judge appointed to oversee the application of a sentence who
is responsible for supervising the penalty. It therefore requires
considerable human resources in the form of administrative
personnel in order to be effective. This makes it rather costly in
practice; but it is very positive in the sense that people can be
punished without taking them away from their work and family,
making them pay in a different way for the harm they have caused.

In developing countries, community service appeared as a
formal alternative to prison in the early 1990s, even though it
already existed in many traditional communities. The first large-
scale exercise took place in Zimbabwe, with PRI's support. The
law had first of all to be changed so as introduce community
service into the penal code and specify what offences it could apply
to – generally, minor offences punishable by at most one year in
prison. A national committee, chaired by a judge and including
members of the legal professions, police, specialist NGOs and
community leaders, was then formed to get this new system
working. Placement institutions likely to benefit from unpaid
work were identified. Schools with no budget for essential work,
public works departments and municipal bodies found this unpaid
labour was the solution to their problems. Lastly, in order to adapt
the system to local economic and financial realities, it was based
on voluntary service. Volunteers, some of whom may be justice or
police officers doing this work in addition to their paid job,
oversee the work of those sentenced to community service orders.
Between early 1994 and November 2000, over 32,000 convicted
offenders benefited from this form of alternative sentence in
Zimbabwe.

In 1996, the National Committee analysed the reasons for this
success. In the first place, it was political will that counted, but the
magistrates also played a crucial part, to the extent that any
reform of the system is doomed to failure if they are not included
in it. The third factor was the growth of a civil society open to
debate, and willing to take an active part in the reform movement.
In fact, no public service body, however well-endowed, would be
able to succeed in such an undertaking without such extra help.

The experience has been repeated in a dozen other African
countries, and exported to Latin America and both Central and

Eastern Europe. In Brazil, prison sentences of up to four years may be commuted to community service. In Rwanda, the second-rank génocidaires are now being given this kind of sentence. The general recourse to voluntary oversight has allowed these alternatives to function without waiting for weighty budget allocations to become available and without cumbersome state structures. In a number of countries, government officials were initially sceptical about the effectiveness of this system. Thanks once again to voluntary work, we were able to set up pilot projects to demonstrate its worth.

After many false starts and problems of all kinds, community service seems now to have taken off. In countries such as Kenya, it took a long time to find its niche within the penal system. Preparatory work started in 1995, but it was only in December 1998 that a bill providing for alternatives to prison was approved by Parliament and only in late 1999 that the first alternative sentences were passed. After that, things moved quickly: in 2000, over 50,000 offenders were sentenced to community service. The Kenyan example shows just how important this new approach to sentencing is, in allowing medium-level crime – i.e., those crimes that are not serious enough to prove really harmful to society – to be managed in a more flexible way.

Post-sentence rehabilitation

Prisons are still self-contained, hidden places that society would prefer to forget. Which is why there is an increasing tendency to remove them from city centres. The arguments given to justify their relegation to ever more distant and isolated suburbs – such as the soaring price of land and buildings, or the lack of space in city centres – do not suffice to explain these moves. It is in fact an attempt to keep prisons out of sight and thus out of mind for ordinary citizens. As long as they remain closed places, they will resist all attempts at opening them up to the world. As we have seen, prisons are also overcrowded and badly managed – especially in developing countries – by staff who are ill-trained for their very special line of work. From Nepal to Lebanon, from Jordan to Guinea, detention centres are managed by staff trained for policing and maintaining order, and not for work in a prison environment.

These shortcomings are aggravated by the almost universal absence of penal policies aimed at limiting the harmful effects of imprisonment. By humanising the conditions of detention and making life inside prison as similar as possible to life outside, we may nonetheless hope to reduce its negative impact. Quite apart from the need to respect prisoners' basic dignity, promoting this kind of policy means better preparation for their return to normal life, and giving them the will to reintegrate into society without sinking back into criminal ways. This is why the conditions must be created for prisoners both to want and to be able to return to society. The example of drug addicts illustrates the worth of such work: in their case, the time spent in prison should be used as much as possible to wean them from their habit in a positive manner, by removing all desire to return to their addiction. It is vital that prisoners be prepared for their release, which is a very important moment, determining to a great extent the course of the rest of their lives.

These are the guiding principles that should underpin any rehabilitation policy, and which are as fundamental as crime prevention for the well-being of society. Then, if we look at rehabilitation as the main aim of any prison policy, the time spent in prison need no longer be viewed as a punishment. Rather, it should be seen as taking charge of prisoners in order to help change their behaviour, by leading them to reflect on the import of their actions, and thus avoid their being repeated. The basic premise of this process, without which all the rest will fail, is to allow detainees to retain or recover their self-esteem, which is why their physical and moral integrity needs to be preserved. The other absolute condition to be respected if rehabilitation is to succeed is maintaining contact between the prisoner and the outside world. This, of course, goes right against the grain of current detention practice, based as it is on keeping prisons shut off from society; it is, on the contrary, a two-way flow of contact between prison and the outside world that should be promoted. This pre-supposes a strategy that must, of course, take into account the need to maintain order in prison, but which does not subordinate everything to this requirement. Apart from the segregation of different categories of prisoner, which means, as we have seen, that maximum security measures need apply only to a minority, every means possible should be used to facilitate communal activities and general access to information.

Prevention, non-custodial alternatives and rehabilitation constitute the three strands that should guide any policy for tackling delinquency and crime. In both North and South, we still have a long way ahead of us, but pilot projects being conducted on a modest scale around the world show that this is the way to go forward.

8

REFORMING PRISON

What should be reformed in the prison system? As a necessary evil conceived and created to keep criminals away from society, is it not a utopian idea to think of reintegrating prison into society? Penal reformers would reply that utopian ideas are needed if we want to stop prisons churning out dehumanised prisoners and make them instead places where they can recover their lost humanity. This determination on their part presupposes that we have, embedded within us, a fundamental conviction that 'nobody is bad by choice', to paraphrase Socrates. Offending would then more often than not be seen as taking a wrong turning in life and society's duty should then be to put the offender back on the right track.

However utopian such ideas may seem, they become feasible once we realise that the neglect prisoners experience spells danger for any society. Seen from this angle, the reform of prison systems may be an effective way of improving the overall safety and security of law-abiding citizens. In short, it is an ambitious undertaking, but one well worth while, not only because of its faith in humanity, but because charity begins at home.

Resistance to reform

Reform of the penal system needs to be seen as an integral part of social reform, including as it does judicial reform, with prisons only part of a whole. But multiple points of resistance around the world are hindering many attempts at reform. These come in the first place from law-makers themselves, especially in democratic countries where parliamentarians are first and foremost politicians standing for election.

So, to make progress on reforms, the voters and decision-makers first have to be won over, since political will is a pre-requisite for any decision on reform. Moreover, the need to reform generally speaking does not come from the politicians, but from those within the prison system itself, who have to face up to the crisis resulting from the disparity between its needs and the resources at its disposal. As we have seen, it is the prison management in many countries that has called on the authorities to reform the system. In the countries where PRI intervenes, it often does so at the behest of the prison managers, as those directly running the prison system. They are the ones who see at close hand how the system malfunctions and they often feel neglected by authorities who view them as mere executors, while they feel their concerns should be taken heed of.

But resistance can also come from within the prison service. In 1997, the inspector general of police in the Pakistani state of Punjab publicly accused the prison administration of obstructing the release of prisoners, whom it preferred to keep behind bars in order to exploit them financially. Rotten with corruption, as in many other countries, the Pakistani prison system resists any liberalisation moves in order to preserve its source of income from prisoners, since, as elsewhere, relatives must part with a small sum in order to visit family members in prison. Under the military dictatorship in Haiti in the early 1990s, a tithe was exacted called the 'butt fee': each prisoner had to pay to get a place to sit. The sums thus extorted from prisoners and their families were shared out among the examining magistrate, the police and the prison guards. Families with some means would also try to improve the situation of their relatives in prison by paying.

Petty corruption exists in nearly all prisons, with prisoners having to pay their guards to get even the most simple things. When it comes to obtaining illegal privileges, of course, the going rate is much higher. In Rwanda, where PRI undertook major training programmes for prison staff – usually ex-soldiers – nearly all the prison directors and their deputies were dismissed in 1999, and half of them found themselves behind bars for corruption.

They had set up a whole system of misappropriation by hiring out prison labour for profit. This black economy based on corruption is an important factor in resistance to change.

All the same, experience shows that the prison authorities can push for change, sometimes powerfully. This is the case with many countries in Central Europe, Africa and the Arab world. Morocco, Lebanon, Jordan and Palestine are good examples of this will to reform manifested from within the system.

The judicial system is likewise a major focus of resistance, generally because of lack of capacity, as all reforms require additional financial and human resources. But its inherent conservatism may also play an important part in blocking reform. Judges and magistrates are important people locally and their power can transform them into petty despots. There are legions of corrupt judges in the world, above all in the countries where they are few in number and their salaries are too low to provide a decent living for their families. Where corruption is rife, judges will evidently give priority to cases with the highest premium. Mafias around the world profit from these shortcomings, to say nothing of countries where the administration of justice is subordinate to the political power and has no autonomy, and thus no notion of its intrinsic legitimacy derived from the principle of separation of powers. Its function then loses all value and thus it is no surprise to find it incapable of imagining itself as a driver of change. In fact, it only serves to reap profits out of power relations and patronage.

Against such a background, only strong political will can create the conditions for change. In Mali, the drive for reform was initiated by the political authorities. Several reports on prison conditions in Mali, some of them done by PRI, resulted in recommendations which the authorities have taken on board, even going so far – with backing from the prison headquarters – as to dismiss prison guards found to be ill-treating prisoners.

In Kazakhstan, to take another example, some very important reforms are under way thanks to the joint efforts of the political and penal authorities, with technical assistance from PRI. All the former Soviet republics, taking their lead from Kazakhstan, have embarked on a process of reform. Nearly everywhere in this region, prisons oversight systems has been removed from the Interior Ministries and transferred to the Justice Departments. This represents a fundamental switch insofar as it confirms that the penal system logically belongs to a rationale other than one whose sole function is repression.

When the political will is lacking or is insufficient to overcome the system's resistance, you may find pseudo-reforms or backwards steps. In Jordan, PRI is helping implement a programme partly funded by the EU, with support from the authorities, including the royal palace. The word 'prison' had been officially banned and instead they are referred to as 're-education and rehabilitation centres'. But the reform has not yet gone far enough to change old habits and mindsets: recently, just because one detainee managed to get hold of a few drugs from his family, every prisoner in the country was denied physical contact with their visitors. The reform had thus not been fully taken on board by those in charge of implementing it. In Tunisia too, prison names were changed in the 1960s, but that has not put paid to an extremely repressive and secretive prison system in that country. In over twenty years of existence, the Tunisian Human Rights League has only been allowed prison visits twice. Even countries which are trying to make reforms find it hard to get rid of the supposed requirements of security control.

Outside influences

These examples show that penal reform is subject to the vagaries of politics and international affairs. The desire for change in Eastern Europe is a result of the disintegration of the Soviet system and the end of international isolation. Although economic liberalisation has often had a negative impact, this is not the case when it comes to the opening up of political space. The fact that these countries aspire to become partners of the EU and, in some cases, candidates for membership, obliges them to change their laws, abolishing the death penalty in particular, as well as changing their approach to prison administration so as to conform with European standards. Indeed, they have to show concrete proof that they are willing to respect them. Reformers in these regimes, moreover, make use of these European conditionalities as leverage to hasten the process of reform. Here, external factors and internal developments join forces to liberalise regimes that in the recent past were authoritarian in character.

On the other hand, these judicial and prison conditionalities prevent a country like Turkey from really getting closer to the EU, since its prison system is extremely harsh and contravenes all the international norms governing this sector. Turkey offers a good example of the strength of resistance to change. The army is fiercely hostile, pointing to the danger that religious and nationalist extremists represent. It is so powerful that it can block any reforming tendencies within government. Turkey is a country where the situation concerning prisons is extraordinarily complex. When the government tried to follow European standards more closely in 1999 by installing individual cells in prisons, they provoked a mass protest movement among political prisoners, who accused them of using these norms to increase their isolation and break their resistance. Hunger-strikes have already led to dozens of deaths among prisoners and their supporters. It is true that individual cells are reserved for Kurdish political prisoners or those on the far left, a fact about which public opinion is generally unaware. The authorities respond by saying that communal cells tend to promote a totalitarian organisation of prison life, which is also true. Meanwhile, the hunger-strikers continue to die in the midst of general indifference. This doesn't mean that the need to conform to European standards, for those states who wish to join the EU, is not a very positive inducement to reform.

What reforms, and for what kind of prison?

For a reform to succeed, you have to give it the necessary resources. PRI regularly discusses this issue in its publications, at symposiums and seminars, and in its contacts with governments who call on its assistance. You first of all have to have new material and technical resources allowing for a broader understanding of the prison population, with computerised data to make it more easily accessible.

But that is not enough: a complete review of existing systems is not only a question of money. All reforms require first and foremost a profound change in people's mentality. Granting the means for reform is of course a positive factor, but it is not an essential requirement for success. There are examples of successful projects using negligible material resources. Besides, many improvements only require better use of existing resources rather than new ones. It is also more useful to bring the whole of society gradually forward to espouse reform than to focus solely on the issue of resources, which can serve as an excuse for doing nothing – the more so since funding, usually from foreign donors in the case of developing countries, is usually short-lived, while what is essential is to make the reforms irreversible. Over-dependency on donors should thus be avoided. This is why PRI tries to install reforms which require very little financial input.

On this issue, the example of our experience in Yemen is particularly apt. In 1998, on the advice of its donors, Yemen called on PRI to assess the feasibility of reforms and of introducing human rights training into prison management. I went there with a British expert to visit the prisons, make contact with local NGOs and develop an experimental programme in the five main prisons of the country. Under the eye of the prison management, this started by sensitising and training staff in these five establishments with a series of conferences and workshops. After having identified and analysed the main problems encountered and researched adequate solutions, each prison then drew up a practical programme to remedy them. After a time, we were to come back and visit the prisons, evaluate each project during meetings with prison management, the line ministry and partner NGOs, award a prize to the most successful project and popularise it in all the country's prisons so as to encourage them to adopt the same approach.

But just before leaving, I learned that the government had put a stop to all this, following a smear campaign against 'foreigners' – in other words, the West, accused of trying to impose its concept of human rights – and that from now on they wanted financial aid instead to build new prisons. Everything came to a halt. This example shows how difficult it can be to work with governments whose only knowledge of the foreign environment is of financial assistance and loans. Asking for financial help has become a culture that it is very difficult to fight. Habits of dependency can thus ruin the will for reform if it counts only on foreign financial aid to succeed.

A realistic ideal

The perfect prison does not and will never exist. Prison cannot be considered as an independent entity, deprived of context, but should be looked at within the overall justice system, with the word 'system' evoking a complex reality. If we have to speak of an ideal, it would be to see this system, however impoverished it might be, acquiring sufficient complexity to deal with matters fairly and ensure that each individual case receives appropriate treatment.

It should, among other things, have at its disposal high-security detention centres for hardened criminals – who are everywhere relatively few in number – with structures and staff capable of helping them at the same time to become less of a threat to society. The physical separation of different categories of prisoner should have as its complement the notion that every prisoner changes during the course of his or her detention and should be helped to deal with this change. You can see that all this is therefore complex, and that the specific elements of prison life require qualified staff to deal with them. To train them, all it needs is to create centres for that purpose within the prisons. As I have said, there must also be open prisons for those categories of detainees who are likely to move rapidly towards rehabilitation.

When the administration helps detainees to develop, it develops alongside them. This needs a high staff-inmate ratio, as adequate human resources are essential to these reforms. It doesn't mean inflating the office staff at prison headquarters or increasing the number of warders, but putting well-motivated and qualified employees – supervisors, but also doctors, educators, cultural workers, lawyers, etc. – in contact with the detainees. It is a big machine that must be set in motion, which is why it cannot rely solely on salaried staff and public funds. No country in the world can deal with crime using only salaried employees.

Paradoxically, it is rich countries that make most use of voluntary work. In developing countries, on the other hand, governments mistrust civil society to such a degree that prisons are often kept secret, well-guarded and inaccessible to NGOs. This situation is changing, however, as many developing states have come to realise that they cannot hope to do it all on their own. In a juvenile detention centre in Karachi, religious education is run by an NGO, another takes care of legal aid, yet another sends in artists to help the young people develop their talents in painting, drawing, singing and theatre. A similar experiment is being carried out in a detention centre in Tehran: retired educators come there to teach as volunteers. The involvement of NGOs is therefore essential, especially in countries that are unable to mobilise large-scale resources.

In the EU, apart from the Scandinavian countries and the Netherlands, which are undeniably the most advanced innovators with regard to prisons, Ireland, England and Scotland appear to be making real efforts at reform. PRI has close ties with the British prison staff and management, many of whom take part in our activities around the world as expert advisers and trainers.

Winning over the doubters

When a government decides to ask for our help, the problem is already half solved. The Minister of Justice in Benin asked for PRI's assistance, so in 2000 we went there and visited its prisons. We spoke to ministry officials and local NGOs, and held meetings with donor representatives and funding bodies. PRI identified Benin's needs, found its authorities to be highly motivated and so, a year later, a project started up, funded by the French Overseas Cooperation Ministry and jointly managed by the Ministry of Justice, the prison administration, local human rights NGOs and religious associations, as well as PRI. The first phase consists of revising the laws so as to decriminalise certain offences, provide for alternative sentencing, and reform the prison regulations. During the second phase, obstacles to reform are to be identified and an assessment made of the existing structures' capacity to absorb these measures. These plans are prompting lively debate, which itself helps the process of sensitising people about the need for reform. We will then need to assess staffing requirements and appropriate levels of training. All these processes should lead to a reform sustained by all its stakeholders, so there are grounds for optimism.

Humanising prison thus means working over the long term, and this may take different directions according to the country. Here, we must start by revising the laws. There, the priorities are training prison staff and raising the profile of prison-related lines of work.

At all levels, prison staff must be made aware of the basic principles of human rights and good management. PRI considers this to be of great importance and runs an international programme to train prison staff in it. We are no longer content to have training sessions lasting only a few days or a few weeks, and we now prioritise training of trainers, which has a multiplier effect. We have already done this in Nigeria and Pakistan.

In other countries, such as Zimbabwe or Kenya, the key factor for penal reform has been the introduction of alternative sentencing. In Malawi, the main factor to kick-start the process was the multifaceted help PRI provided for the development of open prison farms. Following this, Malawi legislated for community service and then legal aid, which is now run by local NGOs under agreements signed with the authorities. This dynamic process is continuing: to date, Malawi is the only country to have called on PRI to study the issues of homosexuality and AIDS in its prisons.

Although reform of the prison system is an overall process starting with law-makers and ending with post-release aftercare, the entry point for any reform must be adapted to the realities and felt needs of each country. The most important thing is that it should start somewhere so as to grow progressively into reform of the whole system.

Paradoxically, prison – which is part and parcel of the legally constituted state – is more often than not a no-go area for the rule of law. For it is a place where a powerful armed group, vested with the full authority of the law and the full force of the state, wields excessive power over a subordinate population, who are viewed as outlaws and supposedly deserving of whatever they get. These attitudes are widespread, as when Malawi's former dictator Hastings Banda felt free to say of prisoners, 'Let them rot'. Throughout the world, public opinion reacts adversely to prisoners being well treated and accuses activists like us of wanting to turn prisons into 'five-star hotels'. In order to try and change things and limit prison abuse, that place of punishment and surveillance must in its turn be supervised.

Hence the need to open prisons up to the outside world, and it is the state's duty to encourage this transparency. External watchdog bodies should have their work made easier, since inspections carried out by the prison services, although obviously useful, are insufficient and must be complemented by other assessments. Magistrates and judges should also make regular visits to see for themselves what goes on in prison and calibrate their sentencing accordingly. More parliamentary commissions should visit detention centres, as they already do in democratic countries. Lastly, these places must be open to local and international NGOs, which can signal shortfalls in the rule of law, but also welcome good practices.

To facilitate this openness, some countries, such as Poland and Hungary, have created the post of prison oversight manager. In the same vein, the African Commission on Human and Peoples' Rights has appointed a Special Rapporteur on Prisons. Prison gates should be opened to these observers without any conditions or preliminaries, because their presence contributes to the elimination of bad practices.

The state's job should not be to imprison solely to punish offenders. It should ensure better protection for society and the individual, not through repression and chains, but by means of a project of re-socialisation, reintegration and rehabilitation of offenders according to the criteria outlined in this book.

POSTFACE
Simone Othmani Lellouche

Ahmed Othmani was killed in a road accident on 8th December 2004 in Rabat, Morocco, after attending the first day of a conference on 'Civil Society as a Means to Activate Reform in the Arab World'. This meeting, which brought together NGO representatives from across the Arab world, was due to present its recommendations to the G8 Forum the next day.

It was in August 2001 that Ahmed put together this book, *Beyond Prison*, with Sophie Bessis, and it was published in French by *La Découverte* in 2002. Even with the passing of time, it is still worth reading for its wealth of insights.

Ahmed Othmani continued his work as President of Penal Reform International (PRI) right up to his death.

In early September 2001, he led a PRI delegation to the World Conference against Racism, Racial Discrimination, Xenophobia and Related Intolerance which took place in Durban, South Africa, and which Mary Robinson's High Commission for Human Rights (OHCHR) had organised. He was active in the follow-up networking that resulted in the 2002 Declaration and Programme of Action.

A few days later, 9/11 happened.

It was on 11th September 2003 that Mary Robinson signed her Preface to this English edition of the book, just before stepping down as High Commissioner for Human Rights. For Ahmed, this

was a highly symbolic gesture. Perhaps he was overwhelmed by
the honour bestowed on him. He really wanted to see the English
translation of his text (from the original French) – no doubt to
have it read by his many friends and colleagues, but also I think
because Mary Robinson's text had particularly touched him and
had highlighted the international character and importance, as
well as the human dimensions, of his combat.

He had succeeded in attaining a high degree of effectiveness in
his work and those close to him know that he did not spare
himself.

After 11th September 2001, we felt ourselves to be entering a
new period of resistance to protect human rights everywhere in a
world where they were now threatened, in the wake of the fight
rightly engaged against terrorism. We agreed together that we
could and should act, each at our own level.

I would like to mention here some of the main achievements of
PRI during Ahmed's presidency, as well as some that are more
recent, in particular, the Second World Congress against the Death
Penalty, convened by PRI and the organisation Ensemble contre la
Peine de Mort (ECPM) in October 2004, the proceedings of which
are dedicated to Ahmed's memory.

At the opening ceremony, the 11th Congress of the UN
Commission on Crime Prevention and Criminal Justice dedicated
a short documentary entitled 'Making Standards Work' to Ahmed.
Three thousand copies were subsequently distributed to Congress
participants and others engaged in this work.

In November 2004, a three-day Conference in Malawi on
'Legal Aid and Criminal Justice' brought together delegates from
twenty-six countries, twenty-one of them African. It resulted in the
Lilongwe Declaration on accessing legal aid in Africa, later
adopted by the African Human Rights Commission in November
2006 and by the UN Congress on Crime Prevention and Criminal
Justice, meeting in Bangkok in April 2007.

Since his death, numerous tributes have been paid to Ahmed
Othmani – in Tunisia, France, Lebanon, Morocco, Burkina Faso
and Sudan among others. At a memorial meeting held at
UNESCO's headquarters in Paris in March 2005, a letter was read
out from a group of Lebanese women imprisoned in Tripoli,
Lebanon. It went like this:

To *the pure and generous spirit of Mr Ahmed Othmani,*
As if we didn't have enough terrible news in this prison whose
ugliness continually haunts us and where our hearts tremble with
fear for those we love,

Ahmed Othmani, we remember well your last visit some three
years ago and we recall the warmth and hope that shone from
your eyes. The promise you brought for changing our conditions
in prison, for a more humane regime, for more clement treatment
of those suffering the throes of time and society and of those who
were unfair on themselves – this promise remains carved in our
minds for as long as we live.

This brings to mind the adage: The best of men is the one whose
good works live on after his death. The news of your sudden death
brought to our mind all the good you had sown, the efforts you
made to improve our living conditions within this atrocious prison
and to found an association which made hope the common
language in our daily life. Since then, hope has never left our sides.
If it were not for your activism, we would have lost it for ever.

The saddest thing is that a cruel fate prevented us from seeing
you just one last time, from dreaming one last time that great men
are still standing by our side, notwithstanding all our changes and
circumstances and growing difficulties.

The praise we give you can only be from the words of the great
poet El Mutannabi:
I was not aware before you were buried
That the stars in the soil live on for ever

The inmates in Tripoli Women's Prison, Lebanon

His actions are not forgotten, and so his work still goes on.

Simone Othmani Lellouche

Board member of Penal Reform International

13 September 2007